Walking Through Grief

Encouraging Words from the Lord
to Give Strength and Hope

by

Linda D. Miller

TRILOGY

Walking Through Grief: Encouraging Words from the Lord to Give Strength and Hope

Trilogy Christian Publishers A Wholly Owned Subsidary of Trinity Broadcasting Network

2442 Michelle Drive Tustin, CA 92780

Rights Department, 2442 Michelle Drive, Tustin, CA 92780.

Trilogy Christian Publishing/TBN and colophon are trademarks of Trinity Broadcasting Network.

Cover design by: Natalee Dunning

For information about special discounts for bulk purchases, please contact Trilogy Christian Publishing.

Trilogy Disclaimer: The views and content expressed in this book are those of the author and may not necessarily reflect the views and doctrine of Trilogy Christian Publishing or the Trinity Broadcasting Network.

Manufactured in the United States of America

10 9 8 7 6 5 4 3 2 1

Library of Congress Cataloging-in-Publication Data is available.

ISBN: 978-1-63769-802-0

E-ISBN: 978-1-63769-803-7

Dedication

This book is dedicated to the Lord, who has carried me throughout my life and walked with me as I completed His project, and to the Holy Spirit, who provided every word in this book.

Acknowledgments

I am so thankful for the encouragement of my brother and his family, who have always supported me in my endeavors. I also had such great support from friends, especially Ann, who prayed for me and encouraged me from the beginning, and from Linda, who prayed, encouraged, and willingly read my drafts and provided valuable feedback.

Table of Contents

INTRODUCTION

Grief comes upon you suddenly. You don't plan on it, though you know you will face it someday, sooner or later (hopefully later). You can't run through it; it's a process.

Grief is the loss of a loved one: spouse, parent, child, best friend. Or the death of a vision: marriage, business, promotion, dream, finances. Whatever you are grieving, God is there with you. He will see you through and bring you out to the other side. The pain doesn't leave, but it does subside, and if you draw close to Him, He will soothe your heart and calm your soul.

I lost my dad in 2001 to cancer, my mom in 2009 to complications of heart and lung disease, my sister three months later to Alpha-1 antitrypsin disease, a genetic disorder that destroys lungs and liver. Then I lost my best friend in 2017 to cancer. We had rented an apartment right out of college, then purchased a home a few years later. Neither of us married, so we ended up living together for forty-eight years! After her death, I began journaling intently and purposely. Until then, it had been sporadic. I lived in the Psalms for the years during and following each of the deaths. They held life and breath for me. God, His Word, and His promises are my strength. Now I share with you some of what brought me through and continues to bring me through.

These entries and thoughts don't have to be read in order as they appear. Everyone's grief is different. Your need today may be different from yesterday. Do you see a scripture that particularly invites you to ponder? Choose that one. Read it one day or several days in a row. You choose. This is *your* path to walk. Just listen for God's voice telling you which path to choose.

God alone is your refuge and strength. He is your very present help in time of trouble (Psalm 46:1). So start there, with Him, your salvation, your hope, the One you can trust and lean on.

I pray that you will be encouraged and strengthened as you read each of these devotional thoughts.

Lord, thank You for being with us as we walk through grief. Help us to walk with You, not running ahead or falling behind. Help us to trust You through the process, knowing that You love us and will be our strength. In the name of Jesus, who already walked this path, amen.

Walking Through Grief.

He Holds Your Hand

"I am the Lord your God, who takes hold of your right
hand and says to you, 'Do not fear; I will help you'".

(Isaiah 41:13, NIV)

How amazing! The God of the universe, my Lord and King,
takes my right hand and holds it in His. He is Father, Abba,
Daddy, caring for me, His daughter. His message is encouraging: "Do not fear!" He often says that; now, He is saying it while
holding my hand. He *took* my hand; I didn't have to hold it out
to Him, just like my daddy used to take my hand when crossing the street to protect me and keep me from falling. Now, He
takes my hand because He loves me and wants to care for me,
protect me, hold me. Be still for a moment. Close your eyes and
imagine. Can you sense the Lord's nearness? Can you feel His
hand holding yours? Rest in it, bask in His presence and care.

Now He says, "I will help you." He is always with me, leading,
guiding, protecting, helping. He isn't screaming at me. I think
He is whispering, gently reminding me He is my Father, He is
in control, He has my interest at the center of His heart, telling
me, "I've got this." He has every situation that is weighing on me:
car and house maintenance and repairs, medical bills, attorney
fees, transfer of properties to my name, all finances that I barely
thought about before. You name the other things weighing you
down. *In all* these things, He says, "I will help you; I've got this."

He is holding your hand!

Lord, take the stresses, burdens, weights, things that are taking so long to get resolved. They are Yours to handle. Thank You for taking my right hand, for reminding me You are the Lord, for taking my fear, for giving me comfort and courage. Amen.

_____

_____

_____

_____

_____

_____

_____

He's There for You

> "When you pass through the waters, I will be with you; And through the rivers, they will not overflow you. When you walk through the fire, you will not be scorched, Nor will the flame burn you. For I am the LORD your God, The Holy One of Israel, your Savior…"
>
> (Isaiah 43:2-3a, NASB)

You will encounter troublesome times; there is no doubt that life is full of problems. Job said, "Yet man is born to trouble as surely as the sparks fly upward" (Job 5:7, NIV). It's almost like a promise, but one we don't want to hear. We want life to be blessed and easy, but trouble arrives: high waters, rivers, fire, and flame. But God says we aren't stuck *in* them; we will go *through* them, and He is the One who will lead us through.

Difficult decisions need to be made. He is there. Bills flow in monthly, even daily. He is there. Tears flow every night. He is there. Health issues arise. He is there. Often, it seems everything is crashing down, but He is still there. The spring after my best friend died (She was also my housemate, and we had shared expenses), I needed to repair the front porch. The concrete was crumbling, and the rails were wobbly because of it. I arranged to get it repaired. Before I could even get it repaired, I had a leak in the living room after a rainstorm. Now I needed a new roof. Shortly thereafter, my water heater went out. As the contractor was fixing the porch, he evidently aroused a colony of ants, and my kitchen was inundated with them. I had to get an exterminator. On top of that, the brake light came on in my car, and I had to get new brakes! All of this happened in a matter of about four weeks. I felt like I was *in* the flood, but God brought me through. The only explanation for how I had the money and presence of mind to deal with all these issues is God Himself. God was faithful. He always is.

How could I get through trials? How could God even see me through trials? The answer is in Isaiah. He is the "LORD my God, the Holy One of Israel, my Savior." He is LORD (Yahweh): the One present with His people as a personal God, and because He is LORD, He wants to know me in a personal way; He is not a distant being, uninvolved in my life. He is God: the uncreated One who created everything, and because He created me, He is concerned about my well-being. He is the Holy One of Israel: pure, sinless, exalted; and because He is the One and only Holy One, He is the One I worship and the One I go to in time of trouble. He is my Savior, the One who rescues me. And because He is Savior, He wants to walk with me through my troubles and carry me to the other side. Think about it: the One who is LORD, God, Holy, Savior, cares enough about me, cares enough about you, so much that He personally stands beside you, rescues you, carries you, thinks about you as if you were the only one on earth!

He is there for you!

LORD, God, Holy One, Savior, thank You for being all You are, able to do anything and everything to lead me through trials and troubles. Thank You for not giving up on me, for carrying me through until I reach the other side of trials, and then carrying me home to be with You in heaven. Amen.

3

He Is Listening

"But as for me, I will watch expectantly for the LORD; I will wait for the God of my salvation. My God will hear me"

(Micah 7:7, NASB1995).

Did you ever talk to someone and get the feeling they didn't hear a word you were saying? Maybe their mind was on something else. Maybe they were thinking about what they were going to say when it was their turn. Maybe they weren't even looking at you. Not so with God. He hears. His full attention is on you and what you are saying. He's looking right at you and hears not only your words but your heart's intent. It's as if you are the only person on earth.

At times when I was grieving, I felt like I couldn't express myself to anyone and be accurately heard. Sometimes, I didn't even know exactly what I was feeling, or there were no words to express what I was feeling even to myself, but God hears even the words I can't say. He hears my heart, and He hears my groanings, the feelings I have that I can't even express. "For we do not know what we should pray for as we ought, but the Spirit Himself makes intercession for us with groanings which cannot be uttered" (Romans 8:26, NKJV). He knows my heart and the depths of my emotions. Sometimes, I just said, "Lord." I didn't know what else to say, and that's okay because He can interpret what I mean and what I feel by that one word. Sometimes I just said, "Help," and He knew exactly what I needed. He still does.

I want to "…watch expectantly for the LORD and wait for the God of my salvation." I don't want to be so busy doing things that don't matter that I miss what He wants me to see, what He wants me to do. I don't want to run ahead or lag behind, to chase after something good when He has something better. Watching and waiting imply I must find time to be still and listen. He hears me, but I need to hear Him as well, watching and waiting for His best, not settling for anything less.

He is listening!

Lord, thank You that You hear every word I speak and every thought I have. You even hear me when I can't express what I want to say. Remind me to bring every concern to You, knowing that You care enough to listen. Help me also to listen for Your voice, to hear what You say to me. Amen.

_____

_____

_____

_____

_____

_____

_____

4

He Is Your Light

"Do not rejoice over me, O my enemy. Though I fall I will rise; Though I dwell in darkness, the Lord is a light for me. He will bring me out to the light, And I will see His righteousness"

(Micah 7:8,9b, NASB1995).

As you are walking through grief, you may feel as though you have fallen and can't get up. When we fall, Satan, our enemy, rejoices. Don't let him get by with it. Take away his rejoicing by getting up. Let the Lord lift you. You may feel as though you are in a dark tunnel, but Jesus is the light that gets you through the tunnel and brings you out to the other side. You will see His righteousness and all His glory. How do we rise up, and how do we find His light to lead us?

First, trust Him. Trust in His love. He loves you with an everlasting love (Jeremiah 31:3). He only wants what is best for you, so He uses everything that happens to you to draw you closer to Him and make you more like Him (Romans 8:28). Be glad in His loving-kindness because He sees your affliction and knows the trouble of your soul (Psalm 31:7).

Trust in His presence. He has been with you in the past, He will be with you in the future, and He is certainly with you now (Psalm 23:4). He will never leave you or forsake you (Hebrews 13:5). He is so close to you every moment of your life. In fact, He carries you in His arms in the past (Isaiah 63:9) and in the present (Deuteronomy 33:27). He will carry you all your days and bring you home to live with Him.

Trust in His protection. God is more powerful than anyone or anything you face. He will save you, rescue you, and protect you. He protects you in the shadow of His wings (Psalm 36:7). He will even send His angels to protect you wherever you go (Psalm 91:11). I love the cry of the psalmist in 116:7 (NCV), "I said to myself, 'Relax, because the Lord takes care of you.'" He protects me with His rod and staff, just like a shepherd protects his sheep from all their enemies (Psalm 23:4).

Trust in His faithfulness. He will not allow His faithfulness to fail (Psalm 89:33). You can count on Him to be there for you no matter what happens. When Jesus went with His disciples in a boat to reach the other side of the lake, a huge storm came up, and waves began filling the boat. The disciples woke Jesus, who was sleeping through the storm, and asked, "Don't you care that we're drowning?" The disciples were panicked, but Jesus was there. He was in the boat with them, and He is in any boat you find yourself in. He is faithful and will fight for you to protect you from every storm.

Second, keep praying. Pray without ceasing; pray when you don't feel like it. Pray when you don't know what to say. Pray for wisdom, for strength, for God's grace. Pray for His guidance through the coming days. Pray for others and pray with thanksgiving (Philippians 4:6). Listen for Him to respond to you. He hears you, and He will bring you out of the darkness and into the light.

Next, stay in His Word. Go to His Word daily, even when you don't feel like it. It is the source of your strength, and it will renew your strength. His Word is a lamp for your feet and a light for your path (Psalm 119:105), providing illumination to bring you out to the light so you can see Him in all His glory.

Another important thing is to praise Him, sing, and listen to encouraging music. There are many scriptures about praise. Get out your Bible and do a search of keywords: praise, sing, rejoice. Here are a few to get you started:

- "Come before His presence with singing" (Psalm 100:2, NKJV).
- "Sing to God, sing praises to his name…" (Psalm 68:4, NKJV)
- "Sing to him, sing praises to him; tell of all his wondrous works!" (1 Chronicles 16:9, ESV)
- "Sing to the Lord; praise the Lord!" (Jeremiah 20:13, NKJV)
- Psalm 150. Praise the Lord (the whole chapter is about praising Him).
- "I will bless the Lord at all times; His praise shall continually be in my mouth" (Psalm 34:1, NKJV).
- "Sing praises to the Lord, for he has done gloriously…" (Isaiah 12:5, ESV)
- "Rejoice in the Lord always: and again I say, Rejoice" (Philippians 4:4, KJV).
- "Fear not, O land; be glad and rejoice, for the Lord has done great things!" (Joel 2:21, ESV)
- "…let us be glad and rejoice in his salvation" (Isaiah 25:9, ESV).

Last, reach out to others. It is easy to want to be isolated, to withdraw from society in general, and maybe even from family and friends. However, God has given Christians a family of believers who are ready to come alongside us, pray with us, and be there for us. Sometimes, it is just comforting to know someone is praying for me. Seek out some special people in your life and ask them to hold you up in prayer. I have three very close friends who pray for me because they love me and want what's best for me. I know they are praying for me, so if I am feeling alone, I reach out to them and just ask for prayer. I don't have to say any more than that. I know they will faithfully pray. In addition, I have several people I pray for regularly. As I pray for them, I am encouraged as well.

Though you may be in darkness, He is your light.

Lord, thank You that You are with me in this time of my life, providing the light I need to get through to the other end of the tunnel. Thank You for Your love, Your presence, Your protection, and Your faithfulness. Thank You that You hear me when I pray, and You have given Your Word to provide light for my journey. In the name of Jesus, the One who is with me in the boat, amen.

_____

_____

_____

_____

_____

_____

_____

5

He Has Plans for You

"For I know the plans that I have for you, declares the Lord, plans for welfare and not for calamity to give you a future and a hope".

(Jeremiah 29:11, NASB1995)

From my journal, August 9, 2017 (a little over a month after my friend passed away):

I am on a new journey. Forty-eight years living with my friend, and now she is gone. A big hole is left. I need the hole to be filled, and I know God is filling it. I have not passed this way before; retired, time on my hands (after devoting months of care for my friend), and anticipating God has something still planned for me at age seventy. I am waiting, listening ("Be still and know…" [Psalm 46:10, NKJV]). Show me, Lord, who You are and what You want. Carry me. "Lead me in the right path, O God, or my enemies will conquer me [enemies of despair, discouragement, impatience, weakness]. Make Your way plain for me to follow" (Psalm 5:8, NLT).

God has stayed near to me, closer than I can even imagine. He continues to lead, but sometimes I have gone off on my own, chasing this thought or idea, thinking He may want me to do this or that. However, if I'm headed the wrong way, He always stops me. He makes my plans null and void, so I go back to Him, listening again. I went through a long period of time when I couldn't discern anything He wanted me to do. I kept listening and finally heard Him say, "Wait." I made it my goal to wait for Him, to rest in Him, draw closer to Him, get to know Him more intimately. I know all He wanted from me for that time was just to wait. It wasn't easy; I wanted to be busy for Him.

He has plans for me, and He knows what those plans are. They have been there since before I was born (Psalm 139:16). He isn't just now making them up or just now deciding it is a good time to make them known. He knows His plans for me. And they are good plans for my welfare, future, and hope. Though grief may grip me, He is using it as part of His plan. He saw death and grief coming; they did not catch Him by surprise. He was there with me, and He continues to be with me now, holding me, working out His plans for me. He still wants me to wait for Him and spend more time with Him, drawing closer to Him, getting to know Him more intimately. That part of His plan hasn't changed. I continue to seek Him, to trust Him, to wait on Him. He is still working out His plans for me; He isn't finished with me yet.

He has plans for you!

Thank You, Lord, that You have plans for me, that You aren't finished with me, and everything that comes into my life is part of Your plan. Your plans are good and promise a future and a hope. Help me when I get restless and run ahead of You. Help me to wait on You. Amen.

6

God, Our Refuge, Strength, Help

"God is our refuge and strength, a very present help in trouble. Therefore, we will not fear, even though the earth be removed, and though the mountains be carried into the midst of the sea; though its waters roar and be troubled, though the mountains shake with its swelling".

(Psalm 46:1-3, NKJV)

When the unexpected happens, it's easy to go into anxiety mode, to feel distressed and overwhelmed with the sudden change of events. But that's when it is especially important to be still, to go to Him, to wait on Him, and to trust in Him. It's okay to have that uneasy feeling, but it's not okay to stay there. He is there to get us back on track.

God is our refuge, our strength, our help. We can run to Him and find Him ready to receive us in His arms, under His wings (Psalm 34:7). There is no safer place than in the arms of Jesus, sheltered from everything that can harm us. If the mountains are carried away, if the waters roar, or if the earth quakes, we need not fear; God is in charge.

He is our refuge, a shelter, a safety zone. He gives us refuge under the shelter of His wings (Psalm 61:4). This reminds me of signs I used to see in neighborhoods that indicated homes that were safe. They were places a child could enter and find shelter if in danger from predators, bullies, or anything else that made them uncomfortable. God is that place. He is there as a shelter when anything threatens us physically, emotionally, or spiritually. He even protects us when we don't know we are in danger. One time a driver lost control of his car and headed straight for me in my front yard. I didn't know which way to go because he was driving so erratically. God rescued me. I didn't have time to call out for His protection; I believe an angel lifted me and carried me out of the way. When it was over, my purse was lying between the tire tracks he left. What a God we serve! He provides refuge even when we don't know we are in need. He is my safety zone, and He is yours as well.

God is our strength. There is no one as strong as He; He has the strength to create all that is around us and the strength to hold it all together (Colossians 1:17). His arms are strong enough to hold us (Psalm 139:10). He never grows weary; when we have nothing left to give, He increases our strength. In fact, He renews our strength as we wait on Him, giving strength to fly, to run without growing weary, and to walk without fainting (Isaiah 40:28-31). There is no enemy, no force, no evil that is too strong for Him to vanquish. He conquers all our fears and all our enemies. He did this time and time again for the Israelites, for the apostles, and He does it for us. If God is for us, nothing can stand against us (Romans 8:31).

God is our help, the One who comes alongside, walks with us, even carries us. The Lord is "…the shield of your help, and the sword of your triumph!" (Deuteronomy 33:29, ESV) As He helped Israel throughout the Old Testament, He helps us today. After God rescued Israel from the Philistines, Samuel took a stone and set it up and called it "Ebenezer," meaning "…Till now the Lord has helped us" (1 Samuel 7:12, ESV). It was a reminder that the Lord was always there to help. He is still our Ebenezer:

He doesn't turn His back on us; He rushes in to help! Do you have an Ebenezer, a reminder of how the Lord rescued you in the past? Maybe it's scripture verses you have hung in your house as a reminder of His presence or a photo of an event. Just remember that He is your help.

God is always with us; He just wants us to come to Him, to rest in Him, be still in Him, and trust Him. He wants us to seek Him as our refuge, our strength, our help, to stop relying on ourselves and hold fast to Him. He is able to shelter and protect us.

He is our refuge and strength, a very present help in time of need.

Father, thank You for being all I need, for being a safety zone from all that troubles me, for being my strength when I am weak, especially now as I walk through this path You have laid out for me. I know You are more than able to conquer all my fears and all my enemies. And Your strength will carry me. Thank You in the name of Your precious Son. Amen.

_____

_____

_____

_____

_____

_____

_____

7

You Are Not Alone

"It is the LORD who goes before you. He will be with you; He will not leave you or forsake you. Do not fear or be dismayed".

(Deuteronomy 31:8, ESV)

Fear can be gripping, even paralyzing, especially if we feel like we are facing it alone. But we are not facing it alone. God has promised to be with us, so we do not have to be afraid. In fact, He doesn't want us to be afraid, not at all. He wants us to trust Him with whatever we face. The Bible is full of promises, and many of them involve God's intervention in times of fear.

The Israelites faced many dangers and many enemies. Like us, they were prone to be afraid. God frequently had to remind them not to be afraid. In Exodus 14, the Israelites had been freed from Egypt. Pharaoh regretted letting them go, so he went after them with six hundred chariots! The Israelites arrived at the Red Sea, with the mountains around them, the Red Sea before them, and Pharaoh on their heels. There was no escape, or so they thought. Moses told the people, "Do not be afraid. Stand firm and you will see the deliverance the LORD will bring you today. The Egyptians you see today you will never see again. The LORD will fight for you…" (verses 13-14, NIV). God then told Moses to move forward; He parted the Sea, and the people walked across on dry land! Furthermore, when Moses gave details about the Lord's laws and commandments, one of the principles for warfare was to "...not be afraid as you go out to fight your enemies...! Do not lose heart or panic or tremble before them. For the LORD your God is going with you! He will fight for you against your enemies, and He will give you victory" (Deuteronomy 20:3-4, NLT). Do you face an impossible situation? Are you surrounded by mountains you can't climb and seas you can't cross? *Do not fear.* The Lord goes before you. He is your salvation. He will fight for you and give you victory!

When Israel arrived at the promised land, Moses sent spies to check out the land. Ten spies came back with a report that they would not be able to take the land (Numbers 13:17-31). However, Joshua and Caleb boldly said, "...do not fear the people...The Lord is with us; do not fear them" (Numbers 14:9, ESV). What a difference in perspective! Unfortunately, the people continued to rebel and refused to enter the promised land, resulting in forty years of wandering. Their lives would have been so different if they had only trusted God and obeyed. God has great things planned for you. Are you too afraid to move forward and receive them? He is with you. Do not fear what lies ahead!

When God commissioned Joshua as the new leader of Israel, besides telling Joshua to obey all that Moses had commanded, He told Joshua to "Be strong and courageous. Do not be frightened, and do not be dismayed, for the LORD your God is with you wherever you go" (Joshua 1:9, ESV). Joshua trusted God, and God worked in Israel to conquer the land which He had promised them. Are you facing problems, decisions, issues you think are impossible, and you can't do it alone? He has already promised to conquer them for you. Just trust Him.

Do you think all these promises are only for the Old Testament, for the Israelites? In the New Testament, Jesus promises these same things and more. In John, He says, "Let not your heart be troubled, neither let it be afraid" (14:27, NKJV) and, "In the world you will have tribulation; but be of good cheer, I have overcome the world" (16:33, NKJV). When the disciples were afraid in the storm at sea, He said, "Why are you fearful…?" (Matthew 8:26, NKJV) When He came walking to them on water, they called out in fear, and He responded, "It is I; do not be afraid" (Matthew 14:27, NKJV). Second Timothy 1:7 (NKJV) tells us, "…God has not given us a spirit of fear, but of power, and of love, and of a sound mind." 1 John 4:18 (NIV) reminds us, "There is no fear in love; But perfect love drives out fear…" Hebrews 13:5-6 (GNT) tells us to be satisfied with what we have (in other words, we have everything we need) because God has said, "I will never leave you; I will never abandon you," so we can boldly say, "The Lord is my helper, I will not be afraid. What can anyone do to me?"

Are you facing something fearful? Not sure where to go next? Not sure how to handle today's problems? Not sure you have everything you need? Do not fear. He is with you. He will not leave you or forsake you. Trust Him to care for you. He loves you and will not let you go through anything by yourself.

You are not alone!

Father, thank You for all Your promises about being with us, helping us, and conquering fear. Help us to trust You and You alone. Help us to remember all Your promises, how you kept Your promises in the past and will continue to do so. You are with us and will never leave us. Amen.

8

You Have Already Won the Battle

"You have armed me with strength for the battle; You have subdued my enemies under my feet".

(Psalm 18:39, NLT)

You are in a battle. Satan wants to destroy you. He wants to knock you out with grief, with despair, with hopelessness. He wants to abolish your faith, your ministry, your hope for a future. The good news is it's not your battle; it's God's! He has already armed you for the battle, and He has already subdued Satan and all other enemies under your feet. You are ready for the battle, and you have already won. The victory is yours.

When Goliath was taunting the Israelites (1 Samuel 17) and they cowered in fear, David chose to take up the charge. He took only a slingshot and five stones to the battle. How can you fight such a formidable enemy with such meager weapons? David gives us the answer. He faced Goliath and said, "…the Lord will deliver you into my hand…then all this assembly shall know that the Lord does not save with sword or spear; for the battle is the Lord's…" (verse 46-47, NKJV). God is with you as well. In fact, He's not only with you but in you. In Acts, Jesus promised we would receive power when the Holy Spirit came to dwell within us (1:8). The same power that raised Jesus from the dead is the same "…incomparably great power…" that is in us (Ephesians 1:19, NIV)! Your strength may be meager, your weapons may be few, but the power you have is great. Your power comes from God, and the battle is His to win.

Joshua faced a strong enemy in Jericho (Joshua 6). It was a strong fortress, securely shut. Joshua had thousands of men he could have commanded to fight the battle. However, that wasn't God's plan. God told Joshua to have all the men of war march around Jericho one time each day for six days. Then on the seventh march around seven times, have the priests blow the trumpets, then have everyone give a shout. What a battle plan! But it worked. The walls fell down flat, and the people of Israel were victorious. No weapons, no fighting, just walking, blowing trumpets, and shouting. You don't need a strong army to fight for you when you have the Lord on your side. He is the mighty warrior. He has everything under control.

In 2 Chronicles 20, Jehoshaphat faced a great army coming against Judah. He called out to the Lord, acknowledging Him as the ruler over all, and said, "…we have no power against this great multitude that is coming against us; nor do we know what to do, but our eyes are upon You" (verse 12, NKJV). The Spirit came upon Jahaziel, and he told the people what God told him to say, "Do not be afraid nor dismayed because of this great multitude, for the battle is not yours, but God's." Furthermore, he told them they would not need to fight in the battle; just stand still and see God work (verses 15-17, NKJV). Everyone worshiped and praised the Lord. They got up the next morning and went out. Jehoshaphat appointed singers to go before the army, singing to the Lord and praising His beauty and holiness. As they sang, the Lord ambushed the armies of the enemy, and when they got to the battleground, there were only corpses. No one had escaped (21-24). They again praised and worshiped the

Lord. The key to this victory was trusting God and also praising Him. They praised Him before battle, in the midst of battle, and after the victory.

Praise is also a key for us as we fight our battles. Praise Him for what He has done, for what He is doing, and for what He is going to do. When we praise Him, there is no room for fear or doubt, for despair or hopelessness. There is no room for Satan when we are filled and surrounded by God. Praise Him for what He is doing, regardless of the circumstances and how bad it looks.

Praise Him now:

> Praise the Lord! Praise God in His sanctuary; praise Him in His mighty heavens.
>
> Praise Him for His acts of power; praise Him for His surpassing greatness.
>
> Praise Him with the sounding of the trumpet, praise Him with the harp and lyre,
>
> Praise Him with timbrel and dancing, praise him with the strings and pipe,
>
> Praise him with the clash of cymbals, praise him with resounding cymbals.
>
> Let everything that has breath praise the Lord. Praise the Lord!
>
> Psalm 150 (NIV)

"Hear this, you kings! Listen, you rulers! I, even I, will sing to the Lord; I will praise the Lord, the God of Israel, in song" (Judges 5:3, NIV).

"I called to the LORD, who is worthy of praise, and have been saved from my enemies" (2 Samuel 22:4, NIV).

"Sing to him, sing praise to him; tell of all his wonderful acts" (1 Chronicles 16:9, NIV).

"I will rejoice and be glad in Your lovingkindness, Because You have seen my affliction; You have known the troubles of my soul" (Psalm 31:7, NASB1995).

He will be praised forever:

"You are worthy, our Lord and God, to receive glory and honor and power, for you created all things, and by your will they were created and have their being" (Revelation 4:11, NIV).

"Praise and glory and wisdom and thanks and honor and power and strength be to our God for ever and ever" (Revelation 7:12, NIV).

> Great and marvelous are Your deeds, Lord God Almighty. Just and true are Your ways, King of the nations. Who will not fear You, Lord, and bring glory to Your name? For You alone are holy. All nations will come and worship before you, for your righteous acts have been revealed.
>
> Revelation 15:3-4 (NIV)

You are armed for battle, and you have already won!

Lord, thank You that there is no power that can overcome me. You have given me everything I need to fight, and You have already given me victory. Help me to let go and trust You to win my battles. Amen.

Praise be to the God and Father of our Lord Jesus Christ, the Father of compassion and the God of all comfort, who comforts us in all our troubles, so that we can comfort those in any trouble with the comfort we ourselves receive from God. For just as we share abundantly in the sufferings of Christ, so also our comfort abounds through Christ. If we are distressed, it is for your comfort and salvation; if we are comforted, it is for your comfort, which produces in you patient endurance of the same sufferings we suffer. And our hope for you is firm, because we know that just as you share in our sufferings, so also you share in our comfort.

2 Corinthians 1:3-7 NIV

9

God Comforts You

"Praise be to the God and Father of our Lord Jesus
Christ, the Father of compassion and the God of all
comfort, who comforts us in all our troubles…"

(2 Corinthians 1:3-4a, NIV)

You've just lost the love of your life. Perhaps a spouse, the one
you've been married to for ten years, or maybe fifty years. Your
love had grown deeper with every anniversary. The two of you
had truly become one, knowing what the other was thinking,
finishing each other's sentences, putting the other person first,
enjoying just being in the other's presence. You still had plans,
things you wanted to do, places you wanted to visit. You weren't
ready for this loss.

Perhaps the love of your life was a child, a beloved son or
daughter. All the hopes and dreams you've had for that child have
vanished. Your loss may be a parent or a sibling. Regardless of
who it is, you aren't sure how you will move forward.

The grief goes so deep you can hardly breathe. But God knows
the pain you feel. He is the God of all comfort; He comforts us
in all of our troubles, all our losses, all our grief. He is there in
your midst, "The LORD your God in your midst, the Mighty
One, will save; He will quiet you with His love…" (Zephaniah
3:17, NKJV). I remember times when I felt so full of grief after
losing a loved one that I was overwhelmed, not knowing where

the strength would come from to move another step. But He was there, and I remember His love enveloping me, wrapping me, calming me. He gave me the peace and strength I needed to make it through one more hour, one more day.

His ears are open to your cry (Psalm 34:15). He knows the depth of your loss; He hears your cry; He sees your weeping. He cries with you, just as He cried at the loss of Lazarus. Remember, too, He is the High Priest who understands our weaknesses because He faced all of the same things we do (Hebrews 4:15). He doesn't stand to the side wondering how we feel; He is a God of compassion, love, and mercy. You are not grieving alone. He is with you, carrying you in His arms close to His heart (Isaiah 40:11). Your tears are His; your hurt is His hurt. Go to Him, run to Him. Don't wait a minute to draw near, to be held in His arms and comforted. He longs to wrap His arms around you and tell you He is with you; He will stay with you and give you the strength and comfort you need to breathe, to live, to keep on going.

The God of all comfort comforts you!

Father, thank You for knowing how I feel, for hearing me, for carrying me. Help me rest in You, trust You, lean on You, knowing that You are all I need. Amen.

_____

_____

_____

_____

10

Focus on Things that Are Eternal

"Set your affection on things above, not on things on the earth".

(Colossians 3:2, KJV)

From my journal, December 12, 2017 (a few months after my friend/housemate passed away):

I was in the kitchen today making cookies and listening to music. I was missing my friend, thinking about how much she loved Christmas. She sang Christmas carols periodically all year long. Then I had this amazing thought: she was spending Christmas with Jesus, the One who came to earth at Christmas to save His people from their sins!

We can get so caught up in the present, in the things we're going through, even in just making it through another day, that we forget the eternal. The things we are going through now are only temporary. So we should focus on the things that are forever, the things that we can't see (2 Corinthians 4:17-18).

Christ is preparing a place for us in heaven, a glorious place (John 14:2), and your loved one is already there basking in His presence as well as in all the glorious things He has prepared:

- God Almighty is there, He illuminates it, and the Lamb is the light. There is no need for sun, moon, or stars (Revelation 21:23).
- Heaven will have gates of pearl, foundations of precious stones, and streets of gold (Revelation 21:19-21).
- Our inheritance is in heaven waiting for us to claim (1 Peter 1:3-4), and our riches (treasures) are there as well (Matthew 6:19-21).
- We will have new bodies, complete and whole, not disfigured, deformed, or deficient; they will be indestructible; they won't wear out or grow old (1 Corinthians 15:42-44).
- There will be no more tears, sorrow, pain, death, or suffering (Revelation 21:4). Hallelujah!
- All our loved ones and friends who have received Christ as Savior will be there (1 Thessalonians 4:16-17). We will enjoy them throughout eternity, never losing them again.
- We will live forever. This is our eternal home (1 Thessalonians 4:17).

It is hard for us, in fact, impossible for us to comprehend all that God has prepared for us (1 Corinthians 2:9). Our finite minds can't begin to understand His mind, His love, and His plans, but He has promised He is preparing a wonderful place for us, and He always keeps His promises.

I was very encouraged that my friend (and other loved ones who have gone before me) was spending Christmas with Jesus. If you are particularly missing someone because it is a holiday, birthday, anniversary, or another special occasion, be encouraged that he or she is spending that day with Jesus. It can't get any better than that!

Focus on things that are forever.

Lord, I thank You that You have prepared a place for all my loved ones and me. I thank You that even now they are in Your presence, rejoicing in Your presence and in all that You have prepared for them. Help me to focus on eternity. Amen.

_____

_____

_____

_____

_____

_____

_____

And these words which I command you today shall be in your heart. You shall teach them diligently to your children, and shall talk of them when you sit in your house, when you walk by the way, when you lie down, and when you rise up. You shall bind them as a sign on your hand, and they shall be as frontlets between your eyes. You shall write them on the doorposts of your house and on your gates.

Deuteronomy 6:6-9 NKJV

11

HIS WORD IS THERE WHEN YOU NEED IT

"...these words which I command you today shall be in your heart".

(Deuteronomy 6:6, NKJV)

I am a retired teacher. The second year, I began teaching at a school that included Bible memorization as part of the curriculum. Each grade level had Bible verses that they memorized on a weekly basis. We learned them together in the classroom, and the students practiced them at home with their families. Each Friday, students individually recited the verse to the classroom teacher. This was part of the morning routine. Over the years, I had learned many verses. About fifteen years later, I became a special education teacher and didn't have a homeroom class, so I didn't have access to the same routine. However, all teachers were assigned to partners for devotions and prayer and were encouraged to memorize and recite verses to the partner. I admit I was not as successful at memorizing and recalling. Fast forward about twenty years when I was teaching at the college level and truly neglecting memorizing. I still had my own quiet time and read His word, but I was out of practice with memorizing.

One day, I was in my bedroom when God spoke to me so clearly it seemed audible. He said, "Linda, troublesome times are coming, and you need to have My Word in your heart. Get back to memorizing." I immediately decided to obey; this was serious.

I wasn't sure what troublesome times were coming, but I knew I needed to be ready. I started writing down scriptures, especially ones that would be needed in times of trouble, and I began memorizing them. God often revealed scriptures He wanted me to learn as I was having my quiet time. Sometimes, passages seemed particularly difficult to memorize, but those often were ones I really needed later. As you choose to memorize scripture, don't be discouraged; keep at it.

There is no substitute for memorized scripture. It is the sword of the Spirit, that part of the armor of God that is our only offense against Satan and his demons. The rest of the armor is defense, but His Word is used to aggressively attack the evil one and his attempts to destroy us (Ephesians 6:17). In fact, God's Word is what Jesus Himself used in the wilderness to defeat Satan. Surely, if our Lord used it as a weapon, we should also. In addition, God's Word is eternal, one of only two things that are forever: life eternal and His eternal Word (1 Peter 1:25). Memorizing scriptures is rewarding, but I found I also needed to meditate on them, retrieve them when I needed God's intervention, put them on display around me, and share them.

The scriptures become more valuable when I meditate on them. I gain new insights, and I am able to drive them more deeply into my heart. In fact, the ones I meditate on are easier to retrieve and are more meaningful. I can reach into my heart and find a scripture that I need in an instant. Sometimes nights are especially difficult. It is then that His Word is so comforting and reassuring. David said, "When I remember You on my bed, I meditate on You in the night watches because You have been my help..." (Psalm 63:6-7, NKJV). I actually created a document with verses that were especially helpful for times I struggled. I printed them off, laminated them, and kept a copy by my bed, in my car, and in the living room; easy to grab, read, meditate on. They provided a calming assurance so I could rest in Him. (A copy of these verses is in Appendix A.) There is also a promise associated with meditating on His Word: Joshua was told to meditate on it day and night so he would be careful to obey it; he would be prosperous and have success (Joshua 1:8-9). I believe this is true for us as well. The more of His Word we know, the better prepared we are to obey Him, and the more successful we will be, not success as the world sees it, but success in God's eyes.

I found it useful to put the verses I was memorizing on display. God gave a clear picture of this in Deuteronomy when He told the Israelites to "Tie them as symbols on your hands and bind them on your foreheads. Write them on the doorframes of your houses and on your gates" (Deuteronomy 6:8-9, NIV). Solomon told his son to do the same (Proverbs 3:3). I put most of them on index cards so I could have several with me. I put many on a ring so I could flip through them. In addition, I printed verses off and put them in various places in the house. Sometimes when I got an encouraging verse from a friend, I would print it off as well. All these visual images gave me constant reminders of God's goodness, His presence, and His peace.

Finally, share His Word with others. Tell others what you are learning, what you have been memorizing and meditating on. Tell them how the Lord is using His Word to bring you peace and comfort. Talk about His deeds (Psalm 77:12). In addition, teach His Word diligently, especially to your children and grandchildren. Again, Deuteronomy gives a clear picture of the importance of consistently teaching His laws and commandments: "…talk of them when you sit in your house, when you walk by the way, when you lie down and when you rise up" (Deuteronomy 6:7, NKJV). That pretty much sums up a whole day. God wants the next generation and all future generations to remember Him, to remember what He said and what He has done (Psalm 78:4-8). The goal is to make God's Word so much of your very being that it naturally comes to mind when you need it, that it flows out of your mouth, that it informs others of His promises and work. I certainly have a long way to go, but it is easier to share and teach when His Words are in my heart. Remember, His Word will not return to Him empty; it will accomplish what He wants it to accomplish, and it will achieve all the purposes He desires (Isaiah 55:11).

Keep memorizing and meditating, and then His Word will be there when you need it.

Lord God, I thank You for Your Word. I thank You that when You ask us to memorize it and meditate on it, You give us the ability to do so. Thank You that Your Word is our delight, and thank You for all the encouragement and comfort You give as we meditate on it. Amen.

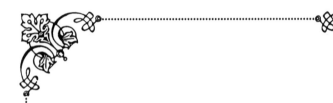

Take up the whole armor of God:

the belt of truth

the breastplate of righteousness

the shoes of the gospel of peace

the shield of faith

the helmet of salvation

the sword of the Spirit, which is the word of God.

Ephesians 6:13-17, ESV

12

CALL ON HIM, AND HE WILL SAVE YOU

"As for me, I shall call upon God, And the LORD will save me".

(Psalm 55:16, NASB)

David is in anguish in Psalm 55. Fear, trembling, and horror are overwhelming him. He says he wishes he had wings to fly away or that he could escape and find a refuge. I'm sure you've felt that way, overwhelmed and distracted, just wanting to get beyond where you are. David continues with a description of his circumstances and the need to get away, but he realizes the solution: I will call on God, and He will save me.

By what authority and power does God get us out of circumstances where we feel so crushed and beaten? Some answers lie in another Psalm of David, chapter 18, verses 1-3. These verses provide vivid pictures of God's power and protection: rock, fortress, savior, my God, shield, horn of salvation, stronghold. By the time I get to the end of all these verses and the descriptions of who God is, I want to stand and shout, "Hallelujah!"

God is a rock, a firm foundation. He doesn't shift around or crumble when storms come. He is the same rock that was with Israel in the wilderness (1 Corinthians 10:4). That rock was Christ, and He is with us, living in us today. He is the rock you can stand on and trust, a rock of refuge you can run to and never be turned away.

God is a fortress, a fenced-in place, a place where no one can intrude. He protects all of His children like a shepherd guards the sheep in his fold. Christ is the defense that saves us, the place we can hide so no one can sneak up on us and catch us unaware. He is always there as the fortress to fence us in and save us (Psalm 31:2b).

David called God his savior, but we can call Him the Savior, the One who gave His life to rescue us from sin, death, and hell. We are so fortunate to have a risen Savior, the One promised to us, the Messiah, who would be of the lineage of David, who would rule and reign forever with all authority. We can certainly trust the Almighty to rescue us in time of need. He is our Savior who saves us from violence (2 Samuel 22:3).

He is a personal God, my God, the "I Am." He is the God who saved Israel out of bondage in Egypt, the One who brought them to the Promised Land, the One who gave them conquest over their enemies in Canaan. He is a personal God and does the same for us: brings us out of bondage, to the Promised Land, conquering all our enemies. He is my God, your God. He knows you personally and cares for you as His own child.

God is our shield, personal armor. He defends us against the blows and weapons that Satan hurls at us. He protects us from his close-range attacks and projectiles. Satan and his army throw fiery darts at us, but our shield of faith protects us and extinguishes every single arrow that is thrown (Ephesians 6:16). Satan is powerful and has powerful weapons, but they are nothing compared to the defense of God Almighty. Nothing can stand against Him, not death, or life, or principalities, or powers, or anything else. We are more than conquerors with Christ Jesus, our Lord, as shield (Romans 8:37-39)!

God is our horn of salvation, our power, our strength. When this quality is credited to Him in the Old Testament, He is called Yahweh; in the New Testament, He is called Jesus (Luke 1:69). There is no one like Him to save the powerless. We can do nothing on our own, but He is almighty, able to save by His power and strength. He alone can rescue us from our distress and despair and provide the escape route we need. We can trust Him to save us out of any circumstance.

God is our stronghold, a defense against strong attacks. He is the army who has built a military compound so we can run there for safety from the enemy, and we can stay there safe from harm until the battle has been won. He is the general, the leader of vast armies that fight for our safety and security. There is no one powerful enough to overtake Him. He scatters His enemies by His mighty arm (Psalm 89:8,10), and He will scatter your enemies as well.

See all that God does for you? For you! No matter what you are going through or what circumstances surround you, God is able to lift you up, to rescue you, to defend you against any enemy (including Satan) who tries to defeat you. God wants you to come to Him in faith, full of belief because He wants us to have victory over our enemies. He wants me, and He wants you to step out boldly in faith, following wherever He leads. He wants us to trust Him to give us the victory because He is with us, and all His armies are fighting for us. He loves you, cares for you, and provides for you: He is a rock, fortress, shield, and stronghold. He is more than enough: He is all you need.

Call on Him, and He will save you.

Father God, Yahweh, Jesus, thank You for being all I need to fight all my enemies, both physical and spiritual. Thank You for bringing me out of distress, despair, and grief; for relieving me when I feel crushed and beaten; for fighting for me. Thank You that I can call on You and be saved. Amen.

_____

_____

_____

_____

_____

_____

13

Keep Your Eyes on Jesus

"…let us run with determination the race that lies before us. Let us keep our eyes fixed on Jesus, on whom our faith depends from beginning to end. He did not give up because of the cross!"

(Hebrews 12:1b-2a, GNT)

We are in a race; it's the race God has given us. He signed us up, trained us, prepared us, and encourages us along the way. Regardless of any obstacles that come to us while we run the race, we are to continue running. And there will be obstacles. You would recognize them as detours you encounter or rocks in the path that cause you to lose your footing. Perhaps a storm slows you down, or maybe discouragement that others seem to be faster and better runners than you causes you to second-guess the race you are in. Maybe you should have been in a sprint instead of a marathon. But you are in the race God gave you, so run it to the finish. Hebrews has some encouraging words for runners.

Run with determination. Keep going regardless of the obstacles. Jesus is with you. He already ran the race and knows every inch of it. He knows what you've already faced; He knows what you are facing now; He knows what lies ahead, and nothing takes Him by surprise. He is with you to strengthen you and help you every step of the way. "Because the Sovereign Lord helps me, I will not be disgraced. Therefore, I have set my face like a stone, determined to do His will, and I know that I will not be put to shame" (Isaiah 50:7, NLT). You cannot fail when He is by your side running the race with you!

Run the race that lies before *you*. You're not running s omeone else's event; you're running your own, the race designed for you, the one that uses all the gifts, talents, resources, and training already provided for you. It's the path He has you on, the road He's chosen. It's the track that will lead you to a full life, a life of blessing beyond imagination. He won't leave you in the race you're running because He called you to run it. Don't forget He has promised to stay with you the whole way (Matthew 28:20).

Keep your eyes fixed on Jesus. Stay focused, looking only at Him. Don't get distracted by other runners who might be able to take a different route, who might finish faster or sooner, who might have fewer obstacles. Don't look at the other runners as a model; Jesus is your model. It doesn't matter how anyone else runs the race, only how *you* run it. You will reach the finish line in His time, in His way.

Remember that your faith depends on Him: He planted faith in you, He made your faith grow, and the Holy Spirit continues to work in you, in faith, during your race of life. As you read Hebrews 11, you get an overview of some Old Testament greats. The reason for their success: they lived by faith. They were able to run their races well. There are many more in the New Testament as well. Paul, for instance, says he ran the race and kept the faith (2 Timothy 4:7).

We are saved by faith, we live by faith, and we finish by faith! Jesus was with us at the starting line, and He will be there to congratulate us at the finish line (Matthew 25:21, Philippians 1:6).

Don't give up. Don't lose heart, don't panic (Deuteronomy 20:3-4). Don't grow weary (Galatians 6:9, Hebrews 12:3). Keep on going in His strength. Jesus stayed the course, finished the race, endured the cross, and rose again to give us life. He is there to help you cross the finish line as well. So forget the things behind, reach forward to the things ahead, and press toward the goal, to receive the heavenly prize for which God, through Christ, called you (Philippians 3:13-14).

You're in a race. You will face many obstacles, but run your race with determination, to the end, keeping your eyes on Jesus! And don't give up!

Lord, thank You that You have designed the race I am to run. You have given me everything I need to finish the race well. Thank You for getting me through and around all the obstacles that are in the way. Thank You for being with me throughout the race and for carrying me during those times when I don't have the strength to run on my own. Help me to focus on You and keep running until I run into Your arms at the finish line. In the name of Jesus, the One who already finished the race, granting me salvation, amen.

14

WHO DO YOU SAY HE IS?

"He [Jesus] said to them, 'But who do you yourselves say that I am?' Simon Peter answered, 'You are the Christ, the Son of the living God'".

(Matthew 16:15-16, NASB)

Who do you say Jesus is? What is He to you? What do you believe about Him? Peter declared Him to be the Christ, the Son of the living God. If you have received Him as Savior, you believe that as well. He is the Messiah, the One who came to earth, was crucified, was buried, and rose again. That is the basis for your salvation; that is your way to eternal life, to an eternity spent in heaven with Him. But what else do you believe about Him? What about the present? What about daily living? What about the circumstances you are in today?

He is sovereign (Psalm 103:19, 1 Timothy 6:15). He is the only Sovereign, the King of kings and Lord of lords. I believe it. I also know that He is in control of everything: my life, my successes, my struggles, all of it. Since I believe it, I know I can put my faith in Him, not just for eternity, but for today. I can stop worrying and fretting and have faith that He has it all under control. I don't always do that. Recently, I received a quarterly water/utility bill for over $400. My normal is around $130. I checked around the house and found the basement toilet had been running. Fixed that; problem solved. Wrong! Next quarter, it was over $600! I called the city, but this was during Coronavirus, and they weren't coming to houses to solve issues. I checked everywhere for a leak, had two plumbers come out, couldn't find any reason for a leak. I was full of fretting. I did everything I could. Nearly every waking moment was spent trying to figure this out. I prayed and had others praying; I checked my meter every other day and recorded the reading. There didn't seem to be a problem at my end, not the meter, not the pipes. I kept fretting. I didn't see how God could fix the problem when I couldn't even see what was wrong. The next quarter, the utility bill came, and it was within the normal. How did that happen? It could only be God! Nothing was changed; nothing was resolved from my end; I wasn't using less water, yet it was fixed. Even though I couldn't see a way out, He fixed it. Why did I spend all that time fretting? Trust God! It has been a daily lesson for me. He has everything under control, even my water usage bill, because He is sovereign.

God is a promise keeper. Bibleinfo.com says there are 3573 promises in the Bible; that's enough to feed on ten each day! When God says He is going to do something, He will do it! Many promises have already been fulfilled. For instance, He promised a Savior who would be born of a virgin, die for our sins, be raised from the dead, and give eternal life. That has already been fulfilled. Other promises are ongoing; they are promises that we can hold onto daily, knowing that what He promised, He will do. He promised to be with us (Matthew 28:20, Psalm 23:4). He promised to carry us (Isaiah 46:4). He promised to provide all my needs (Philippians 4:19). Since I believe all His promises, I can stop being anxious and rest in His promises. He said, "Do not be anxious about anything..." (Philippians 4:6, NASB) When life changes, we are suddenly faced with things we need to do that seem impossible. My best friend was an accountant. She not only helped with my finances, but she also did much of it for me. She balanced my checkbook, did my taxes, and managed my budget. When she passed away, one of my first thoughts was, *How am I going to do all this myself?* Unfortunately, my concern turned into anxiety. As time passed, I was able to take on all these new financial responsibilities. God gave me the wisdom and the knowledge to be successful. Why was I anxious? He promised to meet all of my needs. He promised His perfect peace. He is a promise keeper. I just need to believe His promises and act on them.

Whatever it is you need, whatever you tend to worry about, whatever is overwhelming, whatever has you in a state of anxiety, remember who Jesus is. He is not only your Savior; He is your sovereign King, your Lord, your promise keeper, your helper, and friend. He is taking care of you, He knows exactly what to do in every circumstance, and He will do it.

Who do you say that He is?

Jesus, thank You that You are not only my Savior; You are every-thing. You are beside me, before me, in every circumstance of life. Help me to live like You are who You say You are! In the name of Him who is sovereign and keeps His promises, amen.

15

Your Ears Will Hear

"…your ears shall hear a word behind you saying, 'This is the way; walk in it' when you turn to the right or when you turn to the left".

(Isaiah 30:21, ESV)

Words are important. We use them to communicate. We want to use the correct word to convey the intended meaning. When we write, we try to be careful so we aren't misunderstood. Even as I write these devotional thoughts, I sometimes stop and ponder my choice of words. Is there a better word? God is careful with His words as well. He has written His Word as an instruction manual to us, and He doesn't want to be misunderstood. He wants to be clear and concise. I understand that the original text was written in Hebrew and Arabic, and there were some words that are more exact, words that meant only one thing. We have some words that are not as exact as theirs, for instance, the word "love." It can be *agape* love, true love to God and man, as opposed to *phileo* love, which is brotherly love; both translated in English as love. The English translators try their best to choose words that convey what God meant. He has preserved His Word for us, so we don't have to wonder if it says what He meant.

Three years ago, I was introduced to the idea of listening for a word from God, a word that would be a priority for a year, just one single word that He could use to draw me closer to Him. I listened to Him in my prayer life, and especially in my concern about how He wanted me to serve Him. I was now alone and retired and wanted so much to be doing something for Him. The word He gave me was "rest." I eventually understood that He didn't want me to be busy "doing" for Him; He wanted me to be busy "being" with Him, being more like Him, learning to rest in Him, spending time with Him, discovering who He really is, and who I am supposed to be. That year was a growing year, as I discovered a deeper love for Him and His Word.

The following year God gave me the word "pursue." Proverbs 2 led me to pursue wisdom because wisdom has life-long and eternal rewards. According to Proverbs, wisdom gives understanding, reveals truth, provides instruction in righteousness, and offers discretion, counsel, strength, justice, honor, blessing, and much more. Within a few days of beginning to pursue, I knew the Lord wanted me to pursue relationships, to make connections. I had become somewhat of a recluse. I attended church, but I wasn't actively engaged with my old friends, nor was I making any attempt to make new friends. The Lord led me to renew a relationship with some old friends. They were struggling with the prospect of losing their son to cancer, and I was able to listen and offer encouraging words. It was time to share with others what God was teaching me. That's something He expects all of us to do to some extent: tell others what the Lord has done for us (1 Chronicles 16:8). Your focus changes from self to God and helps others change their focus as well.

The final word I will mention is "trust." This word came to me when I was struggling with my utility bill (mentioned in another devotional thought). God had placed me in several circumstances where my only recourse was to trust in Him, but He wanted to be my first recourse, not my last recourse! He wanted me to trust Him with all my heart from beginning to end, from morning through night. That takes retraining, and He is good at doing that if I will let Him. My first instinct is to fix things that are wrong, to investigate, find answers, and seek advice from others. I pray, but I don't necessarily trust Him first and trust Him completely. I start out praying but trying to fix it myself. I'm still learning to trust Him first, and I'm thinking that is going to be a life-long learning experience. The interesting thing is God also gave me the word "wait" about a month later. They really do seem to go hand in hand. Often while I'm trusting, I need to learn to wait. If He tells me something to do while I wait, that is wonderful, but sometimes I run ahead. He wants me to trust Him enough to wait for Him to tell me when to move, how long to wait, and what to do when it is time. Psalm 130:5 (NIV) says, "I wait for the Lord; my whole being waits…" That is a good reminder for me: wait with my mind, my spirit, my body, all of me. It reminds me of lyrics from a Chris Tomlin song: "Where you go, I'll go; Where you stay, I'll stay. When you move, I'll move. I will follow." I need to wait while I'm trusting. If I don't wait, I am moving ahead of Him instead of following Him. The key is to follow Him, wait on Him, don't get ahead of Him, or take charge of situations myself.

Your ears will hear a word from Him, telling you which way to go, what to do, and when to do it.

Jesus, thank You that You not only hear me, You also speak to me. You tell me what You want me to do and when You want me to do it. You have made it clear that You want me to rest in You, to pursue You, to trust You, and to follow You always and everywhere. Help me to make that my priority. In the name of the One who has revealed Himself to me, amen.

16

Great Is His Faithfulness

"Because of the Lord's great love we are not consumed, for His compassions never fail. They are new every morning; great is Your faithfulness".

(Lamentations 3:22-23, NIV)

There is great peace in knowing the Lord is leading in one's life. Before I was even saved, God's hand was on me, giving me direction. Of all the things I love about the Lord, His faithfulness is one of the most foundational. I am confident that He is with me, and He will never leave me. He promises to give me everything I need, and He is faithful to fulfill His promise. I can count on Him no matter what I go through.

When I got my first job as a teacher, my salary was only $5000 for the whole year! Of course, that was in 1969-70, and it was a Christian school. Had I taken the job at a public school, I would have made about double that. But this year, this position provided me with many opportunities to trust God for my needs. The next year I took a teaching job at another Christian school, making a little more but still facing challenges. The school relied on gifts to help meet salary needs, as most Christian schools do. Tuition doesn't cover all the expenses. With the economy in a downturn, gifts went down. When payroll couldn't be met for all employees, the school made a policy to pay husbands of families first, then single moms, then single women. I, along with the other single women, was at the bottom of the list. When payday was late, I had to trust the Lord to provide the money I needed to pay rent and other expenses, and He always did! I sometimes got an unexpected check or opportunity to earn a little extra money. Often, my paycheck came on just the day I needed to pay a bill. His faithfulness kept me going and growing. I had received Christ as my Savior only a year before my first job, and these opportunities laid the foundation for trusting God to be faithful. He was faithful then, and He has always been faithful.

There are many songs about God's faithfulness that I love, but my favorite is "Great Is Thy Faithfulness," written by Thomas O. Chisholm in 1923. Every stanza, as well as the chorus, is loaded with reminders of His faithfulness.

> Great is thy faithfulness, O God, my Father,
> There is no shadow of turning with thee;
> Thou changest not, Thy compassions they fail not;
> As Thou hast been, Thou forever wilt be.

God never changes! He is the same yesterday, today, and forever (Hebrews 13:8). His compassions never fail. You can count on it. He has helped in the past, He continues to help in the present and will continue to help forever; as He has been with you in the past through every struggle, He will do the same today and forever.

> Summer and winter, and springtime and harvest,
> Sun, moon, and stars in their courses above,
> Join with all nature in manifold witness
> To Thy great faithfulness, mercy and love.

All of creation demonstrates His faithfulness! The seasons never change their expected times; the days and months are consistent. He doesn't suddenly decide to bring winter after spring; He won't give you a thirty-two-hour day. Each day is twenty-four hours. All of nature witnesses His faithfulness. Plants producing crops when expected, animals performing their roles to provide food or clothing or meet some other need. You can depend on the times of the days, months, seasons, and all other creation, and you can depend on Him. You can depend on His faithfulness as well as His mercy and love.

> Pardon for sin and a peace that endureth,
> Thy own dear presence to cheer and to guide;
> Strength for today and bright hope for tomorrow,
> Blessings all mine with ten thousand beside.

God pardons every sin. When we confess sin, He is faithful to forgive and cleanse (1 John 1:8). This occurs when we come to Him for salvation and every time after that. He doesn't turn us away, He doesn't get tired of forgiving, and He doesn't give up on us. He promises peace at all times, in all circumstances. No matter what we are going through, His peace is there for us to hold on to. He promises to be with us always to cheer and guide. When we go through grief, He is there. When we don't know where to turn, He is there to guide. He promises strength for each moment of each day, no matter how tired and weak we are. He promises hope for tomorrow because He promises to be with us *through* each circumstance. There is a future and hope (Jeremiah 29:11); there is a bright future and eternity ahead. Plus, He promises thousands of blessings! We can't even count them, and often we don't see them in the moment, but His blessings are there, nevertheless. Start naming some, and your mind will be transferred from sadness to joy.

Great is Thy faithfulness!
Great is Thy faithfulness!
Morning by morning new mercies I see;
All I have needed Thy hand hath provided
Great is Thy Faithfulness, Lord unto me!

His faithfulness is so great, it is repeated often in this hymn. His mercies are new every morning; every day, we start with a clean slate. He gives us everything we need. Why should we fret? Trust His faithfulness.

Check out some other verses that proclaim His faithfulness:

- "Lord, God of Israel, there is no God like You in heaven above or on earth beneath, keeping the covenant and showing faithfulness to Your servants who walk before You with all their heart" (1 Kings 8:23, NASB).
- "Know therefore that the Lord your God is God; he is the faithful God, keeping his covenant of love to a thousand generations of those who love him and keep his commandments" (Deuteronomy 7:9, NIV).
- "I will sing of the mercies of the Lord forever; With my mouth will I make known Your faithfulness to all generations" (Psalm 89:1, NKJV).

Sing it. Shout it! His faithfulness is greater than we can imagine. He has provided *everything* we need. Thank Him and tell others of His faithfulness. Even in your grief, even in your sorrow and doubt, don't forget that God is faithful. He promises to be faithful yesterday, today, and forever, and He keeps His promises.

Great is His faithfulness!

Lord God, I thank You for all the times You have been faithful in the past. Thank You that You are always faithful. I can trust You to carry me today, to take me through my grief, my sorrow, and my weakness, and bring me to the other side. In the name of Him who is faithful and true, amen.

17

God Means It for Good

"As for you, you meant evil against me, But God meant it for good…"

(Genesis 50:20, ESV)

Genesis 37-50 recounts the story of Joseph, the son of Jacob, who rose from one of twelve sons to become the second in command to Pharaoh in Egypt. Joseph had a dream, given to him by God, that he would be a leader. He believed it and anticipated it. He was the favored son of his father, Jacob. Everything was going well for him. However, something went wrong. Things suddenly changed, and his dream took a back seat. His brothers, who were jealous, captured him and put him in a pit. Even as he cried out to them, they ignored him and plotted to kill him. A caravan headed to Egypt came along, so they sold him for twenty pieces of silver. Good deal for them: they could make a profit and be rid of him, rather than kill him and be held accountable for his death. Not so good for Joseph, who was heading for Egypt far from home and family. When he arrived in Egypt, he was sold to Potiphar, a successful man in Egypt. Where was God in his dream now? Genesis tells us, "The Lord was with Joseph…" (Genesis 39:2, ESV) God is at work, even in the direst circumstances. He is in control even when we can't see it or understand it.

Joseph is back on track to be a leader, if only in Potiphar's home. He was placed in charge of everything Potiphar had: his land, his other servants, his finances, everything except his wife. There lies the problem: she went after him unashamedly. He refused her advances, but she kept after him. She wanted him and couldn't have him. He stood by his loyalty to God and to Potiphar. He refused to sin against God (39:9). Finally, Potiphar's wife accused Joseph of trying to rape her, and Joseph was thrown into prison. Now, where is God? Everything was going well again, but he ends up in prison. "But the Lord was with Joseph and showed him steadfast love…" (39:21, ESV) How can this be God's love? In the depths of a prison cell? That verse goes on to say God showed Joseph favor, and the prison keeper put Joseph in charge of the prison and prisoners. The prison keeper didn't even monitor Joseph's management! God is at work, even in our prisons, the places where we think nothing is going right, everything is going wrong, and there is nothing we can do about it. He is there, working through us to bring us through the circumstances.

Finally, a butcher and baker are thrown into prison. They each had a dream and are downcast because there is no one to interpret their dreams. God reveals the meanings to Joseph: one will be killed, and one will be restored to Pharaoh's service. Joseph asks the cupbearer to remember him to Pharaoh, and he is finally in hope of being set free. However, the cupbearer forgot all about Joseph. Where is God? He's still there; it just wasn't the right time. God does things according to His timetable. When Pharaoh has a dream, the cupbearer finally remembers Joseph two years later! Joseph is brought to Pharaoh to interpret his dream and thus begins the process of appointing Joseph to be in charge of everything, second in command only to Pharaoh. Joseph is thoroughly prepared. He has learned to be a leader, a manager, a little at a time, in good conditions and in harsh. Harsh times are facing Egypt, and Joseph knows what to do.

Joseph's brothers meant for evil what God chose to use for good. God knew what Joseph needed to be a good leader, and He knew Joseph would be needed to save his family and all of Israel from the coming famine. God had a plan. Joseph was a huge part of that plan, but it wouldn't play out unless Joseph went to Egypt, went to prison, and then became Prime Minister.

God's plans are not usually what we anticipate. In fact, they usually involve what we don't want. They include sorrow, hardship, even death sometimes. Where is God in all this? He is with us. He is using every circumstance for good. He is bringing us through whatever it takes to make us what He wants us to be. On the other side of the hardship is the blessing He promises. When we yield to Him, He is able to use us in more ways than we would ever anticipate.

The hardship of watching my dad suffer from cancer, of helping care for him, of watching him face death without complaint became a blessing for me. It wasn't what I wanted or expected. It brought many tears and groanings, which I could not even express, but it also brought rejoicing when he passed from earth to heaven, knowing He was with Jesus. God ultimately used my dad's suffering for good. It taught me compassion and empathy for others going through the same struggles. It gave me opportunities to come alongside others going through similar situations. It even taught me about hospice and other resources available to those in need. I was able to share that information with others and make their journeys a bit easier. God uses what seems like evil; He means it for good. In the midst of trials, He shows us His steadfast love and His favor.

God means it for good!

Jesus, thank You for Your steadfast love and favor even when I am in the roughest time of my life. Thank You that You are with me, and You are using this time and circumstance for good. I may not see it now, but I can rest in Your promise that it is so! In the name of the One who is with me even in Egypt and in prison, amen.

_____

_____

_____

_____

_____

_____

_____

18

My Help Comes from the Lord

"I lift up my eyes to the hills. From where does my help come? My help comes from the Lord, who made heaven and earth".

(Psalm 121:1-2, ESV)

Where does my help come from? I have family I can count on. Though most of them live far away, I can still depend on them to be there for me when I need them. I also have some very close friends. They encourage me, pray for me, and are available when I need wise counsel. However, my real help comes from the Lord. He is always with me; He hears every word I say. He has given me the Holy Spirit and His Word to encourage and comfort me. Aside from being my helper, He is also my stability, my keeper, and my protector (Psalm 121:3-8).

God is my stability (verse 3). He is my foundation. He will not allow my foot to be moved; He won't let me slip and fall. He is with me to keep me on my feet, providing a firm foundation. He sets my feet on a rock, and He commands His angels to hold me up so I won't hurt my foot on a rock (Psalm 40:2, 91:12). He makes my feet like hinds' feet (Habakkuk 3:19). A hind is a deer that is so sure-footed, she can place her back feet in the exact place her front feet just stepped. She is able to run confidently and escape her predators. We have that same stability: to run with confidence as we trust the God who helps us. Jesus told the story of the wise man who built his house on a rock. Our rock is Jesus, a sure foundation that cannot be moved. He is the only foundation already established (1 Corinthians 3:11). My help comes from Him because He provides a strong foundation, the stability I need and crave when everything around me is falling apart.

God is my keeper (verses 3b-6). He is my guardian, but unlike earthly guardians, He is with me at all times. He doesn't sleep, He doesn't get distracted, He doesn't go on a trip, and He never forgets about me. I am always on His mind and in His heart. He is my shade, keeping as close to me as my shadow at my very right hand. He is the shadow of a great rock in a weary land (Isaiah 32:2). When I have no strength, when I am so weary I can't take another step, when I can't move forward, He is my rock, providing a shadow of relief, the strength I need. He is the same keeper who kept Noah and his family alive, the same keeper who watched over Joseph in slavery and in prison. He is the same keeper who led Moses and the children of Israel through the wilderness, the same keeper who rescued the three Hebrew children from fire, then Daniel from the lions' den. And He is my keeper! He will guard me all the days of my life and bring me safely home.

God is my protector (verses 7-8); He protects me from all evil. Nothing can touch me that doesn't first go through His hands. Though I may not like it, He has ordained everything I experience. He uses it to mold and make me, not to destroy me. He protects my soul. I belong to Him, and nothing can take me out of His care. He holds me tightly in His hand and won't let go, keeping me strong and blameless until Jesus comes back again (1 Thessalonians 5:23). He protects me as I go about my daily business, my going and coming. He protects at home, at work, in life and in death, from now and even forevermore.

My help comes from the Lord!

Lord, thank You that You are my helper, my foundation, keeper, and my protector. You are with me today, even as I go through difficult times. You promise You will not leave me. Psalm 121 is a good reminder of all You are to me and all You have promised to do for me. Help me to keep looking up to You beyond the mountains, for my help is found in You. Amen.

19

You Can Trust Him

"Though He slay me, yet I will trust Him".

(Job 13:15, NKJV)

The diagnosis was unexpected. She had been struggling with emphysema for several years, but now the doctor thought there might be something else going on, so he ordered a simple blood test. When the results came back, the diagnosis changed: Alpha-1 antitrypsin. This changed everything for my sister, Karen. Alpha-1 is a genetic disorder that causes lung and/or liver problems, and the prognosis is death. Since it is genetic, my brother and I immediately had a blood test done. Neither of us tested positive. I was devastated for my sister. In fact, I felt bad that of the three of us, she had to be the one to get it. I wished it had been me: she was younger, and she had a family. When I got my results and shared them with her, I cried. She comforted me as I tried to comfort her.

Thus began a journey of calling out to God for her healing and trusting Him to do what is best. Within a year, Karen's lungs had worsened to the point she had no defenses to fight colds or flu or sinus problems. She had to be careful where she went and stay current with her flu and pneumonia vaccines. The doctor suggested putting her on a waiting list for lung transplant, but she didn't see the logic in putting good lungs in a body that had a genetic disorder. I agreed though the prognosis was not good.

Eventually, her liver began to fail, and she had fluid build-up in her abdomen, which needed to be removed. The fluid build-up became more frequent as she got further along.

Karen was such a trooper. She stayed so positive; she brightened everyone's day. She brought laughter everywhere she went. She told hilarious stories, and she often made me laugh so hard I cried. I saw her faith grow as she went through this period. She watched several Christian TV speakers, took notes, and shared what she was learning, not just about struggling but also about life principles. She was growing close to the Lord, and we were growing closer to each other. She was not letting death defeat her; she was going to finish her life with a joyful spirit. She passed away about three years after her diagnosis with Alpha-1, but she is alive and well in heaven, walking the streets of gold, breathing deeply, and enjoying the presence of her Savior.

I would not choose to walk through those years again, but I am glad I had the experience of walking through it with my sister, with the Lord beside us. It was quite evident for both of us that we would trust in God, though He slew one of us. He was our strength. She spent the last years of her life growing to know Him more, and I spent the last year and a half of her life drawing closer to Him, especially in the book of Psalms. I related to the struggles and the praises that so are clearly identified as David and other psalmists cried out to God for help and in praise. He sees us through turbulent times, and we can only praise Him as He rescues us. His Word always brings help and hope.

No matter what you are facing, you can trust Him. For me, though He slays me, I will trust Him.

Lord, thank You for the hard times because they bring me closer to You. Thank You for being there as we walk through the valley of the shadow of death. In the name of the One who died so we could live eternally, Jesus, amen.

_____

_____

_____

_____

_____

_____

_____

Though the fig tree should not blossom
And there be no fruit on the vines,
Though the yield of the olive should fail
And the fields produce no food,
Though the flock should be cut off from
the fold
And there be no cattle in the stalls,
Yet I will exult in the LORD,
I will rejoice in the God of my salvation.
The Lord GOD is my strength,
And He has made my feet like hinds' feet,
And makes me walk on my high places.

Habakkuk 3:17-19 NASB 1995

20

HE IS MY STRENGTH

"Yet I will exult in the Lord, I will rejoice in the God of my salvation. The Lord God is my strength…"

(Habakkuk 3: 18-19a, NASB1995)

I would like to visualize the book of Habakkuk like a play in three acts. First, a little background. Habakkuk is a prophet: he speaks to God, and God speaks to him and through him. In act one, Habakkuk is concerned about what he saw happening around him. He spoke to God about the injustice, the oppression, the violence, and even their new king, Jehoiakim, who was evil and allowed the people to follow evil ways. He couldn't understand why God allowed all this to continue. If the law is not enforced, then injustice continues. I wonder the same thing at times, don't you? Why is wickedness ignored or encouraged, yet righteousness is sneered at or even persecuted? God responds to Habakkuk's concerns: He will punish Judah, and He will do so by using the Chaldeans, a violent, wicked nation that doesn't acknowledge God or any kind of law. They will come upon Judah, march through the land, and possess it.

Act two: Habakkuk is astonished at God's answer. Why would He use a wicked nation, a nation more wicked than Judah, to pass judgment on Judah? Judah is more righteous than Chaldea, though they fall short of God's standard; Judah is bad, but the Chaldeans are worse. He can't understand why

God would stand by and allow such a wicked nation to destroy His people. As the world gets farther and farther from God, I wonder how God can stand it. He is more righteous than I, so He must shake His head as He realizes what we have become. Then comes the answer from God to Habakkuk: write down all you are seeing so everyone will know the truth that the just will live by faith (2:4). God is in control, and His plans are perfect. He will do what He knows is best. He sees the whole picture from beginning to end. I don't know what the future holds, but I know He holds the future. I place my trust in Him. He has the history of earth and its inhabitants in His mind, and the outcome is known by Him. God will do whatever it takes to fulfill all that He has promised. In act two, God also reveals a little of the future to Habakkuk: the Chaldeans are an evil nation, for sure, and they will be destroyed eventually by another nation. The mockers will be mocked; the plunderer will be plundered. In addition, the people will see His glory. He is holy. God will have the last word. Wickedness is always judged, and He will be glorified. We can be confident in that.

Act three is like a crescendo in an awesome cantata. Habakkuk gets it; He understands the message. He asks God to remember mercy in His wrath (3:2). He praises God for His splendor, brilliance, and power (3:3-4). Habakkuk recalled God's past judgments when He rescued His people from Egypt and in going before them to possess the promised land. The past intervention provides proof of future intervention. In the hard times, Habakkuk would wait for the Lord to act (3:16). Finally, Habakkuk proclaims that no matter what happens, he will exult in the Lord; he will rejoice in the God of his salvation because God is his strength! Though crops fail, though herds be no more, though my world is falling apart, though it seems there is no way out, though I can't see tomorrow because of what I am going through today, yet I will exult in the Lord, I will rejoice in the God of my salvation.

He is my strength; I can count on Him to carry me through *anything*!

Lord God, my salvation and my strength, I will rejoice in You no matter what happens. You know my past and my future. You have always been with me, and You are with me now. I trust You to take care of me. I rest in Your arms, and Your arms are strong enough to hold onto me through whatever lies ahead. Your strength is made perfect in my weakness, and Lord, many times, I feel very weak. Thank You for Your strength. In the name of Jesus, amen.

_____

_____

_____

_____

_____

_____

21

PRAISE HIM

"Serve the LORD with gladness! Come into his presence with singing! Enter his gates with thanksgiving, and his courts with praise! Give thanks to him; bless his name!"

(Psalm 100:2, 4, ESV)

The Lord commands us to come to Him with singing, praise, and thanksgiving. This is not a suggestion. You may be thinking, *I can't.*

> *I'm grieving.*
> *I can hardly take care of myself.*
> *I don't have the energy.*
> *I am struggling to care for my family.*
> *I feel like I'm in a fog.*
> *I just can't do it.*

It doesn't matter your circumstances. God doesn't say, "If you feel like it, I would really like you to sing, praise, and give thanks." He commands it. Why? He deserves it, for sure, but He also knows that as we direct our minds and hearts to Him, our focus is on Him, not ourselves; not the grief, the energy, the struggle, the fog, or the feelings. In His presence is the fulness of joy (Psalm 16:11). As we spend time with Him, our hearts fill with joy, and it becomes easier to praise Him. The more we praise, the easier it is to praise.

There's a bigger challenge: God doesn't just want our praise and thanks occasionally; He wants it all the time. "In everything give thanks, for this is the will of God for you…" (1 Thessalonians 5:18, NASB). He's not asking us to be thankful *for* everything, but we can be thankful *in* any situation: thankful He is with us; thankful He is in control; thankful for what we have, not what we don't have; thankful for salvation and the hope of heaven; thankful for a reunion someday with those we love. Thank Him because He has blessed us abundantly and will continue to bless us.

As we praise and thank God, we are also acknowledging who He is and what He has done. "…the Lord is the great God, and the great King above all gods…He is our God, and we are the people of His pasture…" (Psalm 95:3, 7, NKJV) He created the world and everything in it. He gave us life, forming us and planning for us before we were born (Psalm 139). He has given us His Word and the Holy Spirit to guide us through life. He is all-powerful, all-knowing, and ever-present!

Creation will praise Him even if we don't. The heavens are glad, the earth rejoices, the sea roars, the fields exult, and the trees sing for joy (Psalm 96:11-12). Jesus said if we keep silent instead of praising Him, even the stones will cry out (Luke 19:38-40). In Psalm 66, the psalmist cried out to God *with praise on his lips,* and the Lord heard Him (17-18). He hears our cries and our praise. In fact, He exchanges our spirit of despair into a garment of praise (Isaiah 61:3)! I want that. I want to praise Him in all things so that He can change all my sorrow into praise.

Come to Him with singing, praise, and thanksgiving. Others will hear and rejoice with you!

Lord, I thank You that You can take all my sorrow and despair and turn it into a garment of praise. A garment that enfolds me, warms me, and comforts me. You have done so much for me. I don't want to complain; I just want to come to You singing, praising, and thanking You. In the name of Him who enfolds me in His arms, Jesus, amen.

_____

_____

_____

_____

_____

_____

22

REMEMBER

"My soul will be satisfied…, when I remember You upon my bed, and meditate on You in the watches of the night; for you have been my help…"

(Psalm 63:5-7, ESV)

Remember. There are things we certainly want to forget, but there are so many things we need to remember.

First of all, we need to remember that God sent His Son to save us. He came from all of heaven's glory to be born as a baby. He lived a sinless life, was crucified, and buried. But He rose again to give us eternal life. What a tremendous sacrifice, and what a great gift! Remember also what God has done as recorded in scripture. For instance, God commanded the Israelites to remember the Passover, the time when He saved all their firstborns from death. He wanted them to remember for all time His marvelous grace in saving them. Remember what He did to Pharaoh in releasing Israel from his rule, rescuing them in the wilderness, and destroying him and his entire army. They knew they were supposed to remember what He had done so they could know He is mighty, and He was with them. But we also know they kept forgetting. They forgot when they had no water, but He still miraculously gave them water from a rock. They forgot when they had no food, so He gave them manna. He provided the manna one day at a time, emphasizing His daily provision. They complained that they only had manna, so He gave them quail. Sound familiar? We remember the story, but do we remember how often we also forget? We forget how He has helped, how He has provided, how He has rescued. Remember what He has done so we have confidence for the present and the future.

We also need to remember what He has done for us personally. Remember the day you called out to Him to save you from sin. He promises to keep us, to hold onto us tightly and never let us go. Remember the times He rescued you, possibly saving your life. I remember, as a child, I nearly choked to death on a piece of candy. Fortunately, my dad was nearby, turned me upside down, hit me on the back, and it popped out. That was God rescuing me and allowing me to live another day. There are several other times in my life where God has saved my life, and I recall those to remind me that God isn't finished with me yet. As long as we live, He has a purpose for us. Sometimes, it could be He wants us to reach out to others going through a rough time.

Remember His character. God is good. God is good all the time, and all the time, God is good. Maybe you are familiar with this response. One person says, "God is good all the time," and the other person replies, "And all the time, God is good." It is a reminder that He only gives good things, good gifts to us. Remember the good things He has done in the past, and know that He will continue to give good gifts. God cannot change. He is the same yesterday, today, and forever. Therefore, as He has been faithful in the past, He will always be faithful (Psalm 146:6). As He has provided in the past, He will always provide everything we need (Philippians 4:19). As He has been merciful in the past, He will be merciful forever (Psalm 136:3). His love is great towards us, and it is everlasting (Psalm 103:11,17). We are His children, and He will never let us go; no one can snatch us out of His hands; nothing can separate us from Him (John 10:28; Romans 8:35-39). Remember He is in control, nothing is impossible for Him, and no evil can ever get the best of Him. As we hold onto His character, we are convinced we are safe in His hands. What confidence this gives us in our relationship with God!

Whatever I face today, He has already taken care of. As I call out to Him, He hears me and rescues me (Psalm 50:15). He wants me to remember what He has done so I can confidently say, "The Lord is my helper; I will not fear; what can man do to me?" (Hebrews 13:6, ESV)

Remember what the Lord has done for you.

Lord, thank You for all the things You have done for me; above all for saving me and giving me eternal life: life with You and all my loved ones who have already come into Your presence. Thank You also for the gift of remembering, of remembering how You have provided for me, rescued me, and taken care of me. This gives me the confidence today that You will continue to be all that I need, whenever I need it. In the name of the One who is living proof that You care about me, Jesus, amen.

23

He Delivers

"Then, they cried out to the Lord in their trouble, and He delivered them out of their distresses".

(Psalm 107:6, NKJV)

The psalmist tells instances when God's people were in trouble. They ultimately call out to Him, and He delivers them out of their trouble. Then, God calls on them to give thanks. This happens several times in Psalm 107. I can identify with this. I find myself in an uncomfortable situation, maybe in dire straits, and I call out to God. He hears and delivers. Then I thank Him. Another situation arises, I call out, He answers, and I praise Him. However, I have sometimes found myself in a place where I have to call out to God continuously to help me for the same trouble, for the same distress. This has occurred when a family member or special friend was very sick or has passed away. It is those times when I feel like I am frequently crying out, "God, help!" It's not that He isn't helping; it's that I need His help moment by moment. My thoughts are overwhelmed with the illness or the loss, and I need Him to carry me, to deliver me from my distress.

The Israelites found themselves in the wilderness hungry, thirsty, and desolate, their souls fainting within them. They cried out to God, and He delivered them out of their distress. I appreciate the New King James wording of "out of." He didn't deliver them *in* their troubles or even *from* their troubles but actually brought them *out of* their trouble. He was always with them in their troubles, and He walked with them through their troubles but then delivered them out of their troubles. He never forsook them. He was ever-present. What a comfort to me as I go through sorrow and grief. He is with me in the grief, walking with me through the grief, and He will deliver me out of the grief. That doesn't mean He gets rid of the grief; He takes care of the grief, comforting and reassuring me.

The Israelites had to depend on God for everything in the wilderness. They had no other resources. That's where He wanted them. It was hard, but He wanted them to learn they could trust Him. The Lord uses every situation, especially the hard ones, to make me more dependent on Him, to draw me to Him, to make me more like Him, and to make me a more useful vessel, filled with His Spirit, His heart, His desires. Going through hard times forces me to depend on the Lord (which is what He wants) and spend more time with Him. He takes what I think are lemons in my life and makes them into the sweetest, most refreshing lemonade, able to quench my thirst for Him and refresh others as well. He is the living water. If I go to Him, I will never thirst again. He becomes my life-giving well, my constant source of refreshment.

God gives me a choice: I can become bitter, despondent, mad at God and life, and complain like the Israelites (and quite frankly, I do all too often), or I can flourish in my circumstances, bloom in the place He has planted me. My wilderness experience creates empathy in me for others who are struggling. It gives opportunity to speak hope and life into others, and it makes me trust Him more. Choosing to flourish allows me to be grateful for what I have. Even if I'd rather be somewhere else, doing something else away from grief and suffering, I can be thankful for what I have, for the years I've enjoyed with family and friends, and for a bright future, full of hope and promise because Christ has chosen to live in me. It even creates a deeper longing for the return of Christ and a future spent eternally with all the loved ones who are already with Him.

When we cry out to Him, He delivers us out of our distresses! *Lord, fill me with You. Refresh me for the road that lies ahead. Thank You for being with me as I walk through this time, for being all I need. Help me to flourish by Your grace and power, and use me as I interact with others who are struggling. In the name of the One who hears my cries and is able to deliver me. In the name of the One who is Savior and deliverer, Jesus, amen.*

_____

_____

_____

_____

_____

_____

What then shall we say to these things? If God is for us, who can be against us? He who did not spare His own Son, but delivered Him up for us all, how shall He not with Him also freely give us all things? Who shall bring a charge against God's elect? It is God who justifies. Who is he who condemns? It is Christ who died, and furthermore is also risen, who is even at the right hand of God, who also makes intercession for us. Who shall separate us from the love of Christ? Shall tribulation, or distress, or persecution, or famine, or nakedness, or peril, or sword? As it is written:

"For Your sake we are killed all day long;

We are accounted as sheep for the slaughter."

Yet in all these things we are more than conquerors through Him who loved us. For I am persuaded that neither death nor life, nor angels nor principalities nor powers, nor things present nor things to come, nor height nor depth, nor any other created thing, shall be able to separate us from the love of God which is in Christ Jesus our Lord.

Romans 8:31-39 NKJV

24

IMMANUEL

"'Behold, the virgin shall be with child, and bear a Son, and they shall call His Name Immanuel,' which is translated, 'God with us'".

(Matthew 1:23, NKJV)

God is everywhere. There is nowhere we can go that God is not there. We know this from scripture: He is not only omnipotent and omniscient; He is omnipresent, everywhere present. This is something I accept by faith, but if I try to analyze it, it blows my mind that someone can be everywhere at the same time. Only God can do that. In fact, that isn't the only thing that blows my mind about God's presence. He has a relationship with His people that is nothing less than miraculous.

As I write this, it's the Christmas season, and I have been impressed by the name given to the child born to save: Immanuel. That name has been the topic of many messages, devotional thoughts, sermons, and encouraging words, especially as we are still in a global pandemic. Immanuel, "God with us," God with us! That is such a personal message. He is with me wherever I go, whatever I do, whether I am aware of it or not. He was with His people in the Old Testament. He will be with you as well, no matter what your circumstances. Even when you walk through the valley of the shadow of death, you need not fear, for God is with you, comforting you (Psalm 23:4). I've been there, watching family and friends who have received the news of a terminal illness and walking in that shadow of death or being nearby when a loved one suddenly passes away for no apparent reason. God is with me, Immanuel.

God is not only with me; He is in me. It is so hard to comprehend how the God of the universe, the highest God, could choose to live *in* me, yet He does. Jesus promised when He left this earth that He would send the Comforter, the Holy Spirit, who would live in us (John 14). On the day of Pentecost (Acts 2), the Holy Spirit came with tongues like fire and filled the disciples. Every believer since has received the Holy Spirit. He fills us and gives life (Romans 8:9, 11). He lives in us and comforts us; He is our hope of glory (Colossians 1:17). God in us, the Holy Spirit.

God goes before me; He will not leave me or forsake me (Deuteronomy 31:8). God showed Himself to the Israelites as a pillar of cloud by day and a pillar of fire by night, leading through the wilderness, showing them the way to travel. He does the same of us. He leads us in the right path, by still waters, in the way we should go. He doesn't run off somewhere with a more important errand; He stays right ahead of us, desiring us to follow. Christ before us, our leader.

In addition, God holds onto me; He takes hold of my right hand and won't let go (Isaiah 14:10). No matter where I go, He is holding onto me (Psalm 139). I cannot flee from His presence: His hand will lead me, and His right hand will hold me (verse 10). Jeremiah compares us to clay in the potter's hand: He is molding us, shaping us, making us what He wants us to be so we can be useful vessels for Him. So whatever happens to us is a part of the master plan for us to be more like Him. This is so reassuring as we go through struggles that we don't understand;

we can trust that He knows what He is doing. God holding onto us, not letting go.

God also hides us under the shadow of His wings; we find protection and safety. His wings provide a refuge until calamities pass (Psalm 57:1). We can trust that He will keep us safe as we pass through rough patches, hiding us from adversaries, blinding the eyes of those who would harm us. God protecting us in the shadow of His wings.

Finally, God is for me. God will fight for me against my enemies, and He will give me victory. That is the promise He gave Israel as part of the law (Deuteronomy 20:4). When they went to battle, trusting the Lord, they need not fear, for God would be with them to fight for them. Romans 8:31-39 gives us the same promise. If God is for me, who can stand against me? The answer: no one! Nothing! Not hardship, danger, illness, death, persecution. Nothing! Anyone or anything that tries to defeat me would have to be stronger than God, and that is not possible. Since the Lord is for me, I will not fear (Psalm 118:6). We can be fully confident that when He is for us, there is no one and nothing that can possibly interfere with God's plan for us.

God with us, in us, before us, holding onto us, protecting us, and for us! Immanuel!

Lord, I am overwhelmed that the God of the universe would come and abide in me: to be with me, in me, before me, holding onto me, and protecting me, acting on my behalf. Thank You that You gave Your Son and that He sent the Holy Spirit to dwell within me. There is nowhere I can go that You are not there, and there is nothing that can happen to me that You have not ordained. I thank You in the name of the One who is Immanuel, God with me. Amen.

25

WORDS OF LIFE

"Lord, to whom shall we go? You have the words of eternal life".

(John 6:68, NKJV)

There are sixty-six books in the Bible, the longest of which is the book of Psalms, the book of songs. It is a collection of songs and prayers that became a sort of prayer book for the Israelites. In fact, many of the psalms, or portions of them, have become hymns and even modern praise songs. About half of the chapters were written by David. Most of the chapters in Psalms are pretty short, thirty verses or less, and a few have fifty to seventy-five verses. However, the longest by far is Psalm 119, with 176 verses! Why so long? This particular Psalm is a celebration of God's law. I just finished reading that chapter the other day. I confess I did not read the whole chapter in one sitting. I actually took six days to read it. As I read it, I jotted some notes in my journal of verses that were particularly meaningful to me at this stage of my life. When I finished, I pondered its length and recognized this Psalm honors and magnifies the importance of God's Word. His Word is referred to by several names in this book: testimonies, precepts, statutes, commandments, and word, to name a few. The psalmist recognized the importance of God's Word in directing his steps, in giving success by obedience to them, in keeping him from sin, in receiving wise counsel, and in other words, living a life that pleases God and results in His blessing.

Something to remember, though, is that all the psalms are not about rejoicing, *everything is great, this is such a wonderful life,* seeing life through rose-colored glasses. Although many psalms are praises and songs that glorify and praise Him, some psalms are cries to God for deliverance, some beg God for His intervention in serious situations, and some even ask God what is taking Him so long to come to the rescue! I can relate to that. I have done all those things: praise, cry out, beg, and question. It's easy to praise Him when life is great, but when life isn't great, it is okay to cry out, even beg Him for quick deliverance. It's even okay to ask Him questions. He wants us to come to Him boldly and honestly, and the psalms are honest reflections of those who love Him but also wonder what He is doing and when He will come to their aid.

As I have watched loved ones struggle with health issues, unable to help as they face the possibility of death, I have cried out to God for healing, begged Him for healing, pleaded for mercy for the loved one and for those caring for him or her. I have asked God how long the suffering needed to go on. God has always been there, providing His grace and mercy on every sickbed. He has always answered my prayers, not necessarily in the way I was hoping, but my faith has always led me to realize His will is best. Though so many of my loved ones were not healed on earth, they were ultimately healed in heaven. I remember specifically thanking God at the moment of their passing for His healing, that they were in heaven able to walk, to breathe, to speak, and to rejoice in His presence. What a blessing!

I am so thankful for the book of Psalms. It reflects real life. I mentioned before that I stayed in the Psalms for many months as people I loved were terminally ill. It was a source of strength and encouragement for me, and it still is. The Lord prompts me back to that book about once a year, and I always find reassurance and hope, as well as opportunities to praise God for who He is and all He's done. I encourage you to go to the scriptures for strength, but especially in time of need, go to the Psalms.

His Word gives life, hope, strength, and encouragement! Go to Christ and His Word; they are eternal life.

Lord, thank You for Your Word. It has everything I need for life and hope. Thank You that You hear me when I call, that I can come to you boldly and even be honest with You. Help me to stay in Your Word, to obey it, to find Your peace in it, and to find out how to live a life pleasing to You. In the name of the One who is the Living Word, Jesus, amen.

26

HE IS MINE FOREVER

"...God remains the strength of my heart..."

(Psalm 73:26, NLT)

I don't like to be sick. I like to be doing things, and illness gets in the way. I can manage through a cold because even if I feel miserable, there are things I can still do. Headaches are painful interruptions but usually short-lived. However, if I get the flu or something else that puts me in bed or on the couch for an extended time, I get really discouraged and frustrated. I want to be well; I want to feel good enough to be up and about. So I sometimes wonder how people who have extended illnesses or debilitating issues manage. How do they get through it long term? I think of Joni Eareckson Tada, who, at the age of seventeen, had a diving accident that caused her to be quadriplegic. She is paralyzed from the shoulders down and, at this writing, is seventy-one years old. That is a long time to be in a wheelchair, depending on others for so many things she does. However, she is an author, radio host, founder of *Joni and Friends*, painter (she paints with a brush in her teeth), and speaker. How does she do it? I believe it is reflected in Psalm 73: God is the strength of her heart. She depends on the Lord for her daily strength, both physically and spiritually. I think that same attitude extends to those around her as well: her husband and her caregivers. They, too, must depend on the Lord for help both spiritually and physically.

My mom had a mild heart attack when she was seventy-four. They had to put in two stents, but she was fairly healthy until she was seventy-nine. She went to her regular doctor for a check-up, and he detected she had atrial fibrillation. He conferred with her cardiologist, who told her to double one of her medications and come to his office the next morning. When I went to pick her up the next morning, she was so weak she could barely move. I had to call the emergency squad to take her to the hospital. The doctors there did a few tests but planned more complex tests the next day. The following day I arrived at the hospital to find her lethargic and unresponsive. The nurse called for emergency help, and it was determined she had carbon dioxide saturation. This happens when the body isn't expelling carbon dioxide enough to get sufficient oxygen. She ended up in ICU and thus began an eleven-month illness, a cycle of rehabilitation, relapse (usually due to carbon dioxide saturation), ICU, back to rehabilitation, and so on. She was even intubated for a time. She was able to come home after five months of this cycle, but she was never able to recover enough to get out of bed on her own. During this time, I wondered how she could manage all she was going through. There is only one explanation: she may have had a weakened heart and weakened lungs, but God was the strength of her heart spiritually. He was the strength of my heart as well. While it is difficult to be sick and bedridden, I believe it is more difficult to watch someone you love go through an illness that robs them of mobility, strength, and quality of life. I had to depend on God's strength to sustain me both physically and spiritually (and emotionally) as I cared for her. She passed away from complications eleven months after the initial episode, but I praise God for His spiritual sustenance.

If you are going through an extended illness yourself or are caring for a loved one with an extended illness, be assured that God is the strength of your heart. He will care for you spiritually and emotionally. I love the rest of the verse, "He is mine forever!" He won't let go nor leave me to wallow in my pain. He cares about every second of my life, every tear that falls, every moment of desperation.

He is mine forever!

Lord, You are my only hope when those around me are suffering from a debilitating or terminal illness. You care about me spiritually and emotionally, as well as physically. You strengthen my heart so that I can endure the pain I see and feel. And You are here with me (and with them) forever! In the name of the One who gives everlasting life and encouragement, Jesus, amen.

_____

_____

_____

_____

_____

_____

_____

Photo by Linda D. Pierce

27

MY OWN PERSONAL FORT

"Be a rock of refuge for me, a strong fortress to save me!"
(Psalm 31:2b, ESV)

Sometimes life is overwhelming. We can become weary, be stretched to the limits, and have no time to deal with things. Our stamina is depleted, and we don't have the mental alertness to figure out what to do. Satan seems to be throwing his fiery darts from every direction. Where could we go to get away from it all? God is our only refuge. Only He can help. We can trust Him to be a place of safety.

Affliction has a purpose, often many purposes. God sometimes uses adversity to bring us to Him or to bring us back to His Word. He can use it to teach us His ways or to show us His faithfulness. Sounds good on paper or makes sense for someone else, but when I'm in the midst of the affliction, I want answers. When trouble comes, I want out! I want to flee! Life is hard just getting through the demands of daily things, but when you add illness, or death of a loved one, or a broken relationship, or financial difficulties to it, it seems insurmountable.

Psalm 139:5 says God encloses me behind and before and lays His hand on me. David often was surrounded by enemies, including King Saul. In Psalm 31, he asks God to be his fortress, his rock of safety. And God was that fortress and rock of safety. God saved David countless times from his enemies.

I can picture a fortress with a roof on top surrounding me. He has me so enclosed in His care; it's like having my own personal fort. It's a place of safety. He guards the door so nothing and no one can get in. Anything that comes into my life has already passed through His hands, through the gate of the fort. How can anything harm me? It can't! This truth doesn't change the circumstances, but it sure changes my outlook. I can face anything when I know He is my fort, with me, surrounding me, holding me, and guarding the door against all enemies.

You have that same fort with Jesus guarding the door. No one and nothing can harm you because you are safe under His watch. You can trust Him to care for you, intercede for you, and protect you. He will hold you and keep you securely in His arms.

Our afflictions, our scary circumstances, are part of God's plans for us. These trials should cause us to run to Him, to call out to Him, to rest in Him, and to trust Him for everything that happens to us. The result can be getting to know Him better, drawing closer to Him, learning His ways and His character more fully. These are immeasurable benefits. Our trials are brief compared to eternity, but the rewards of Christ's presence with us are eternal.

Life can be overwhelming, but you have a place of safety, a personal fort!

Lord, thank You for being my fort, my refuge. Help me to keep my focus on You and not on the circumstances; help me to remember there is no way any enemy can get through or around You. I am secure in the One who cares for me more than anyone else. Amen.

28

Through Tribulation to Hope

"...we also celebrate in our tribulations, knowing that tribulation brings about perseverance; and perseverance, proven character; and proven character, hope".

(Romans 5:3-4, NASB)

The book of Romans is a great foundational book for Christians. It provides the basis for salvation: all have sinned; the wages of sin is death; the gift of God is eternal life through Christ; we are justified by faith; there is no condemnation when we are in Christ. In addition, Romans clarifies that we are God's children, and He is a loving Father. Finally, we are assured that God's love is poured out on us in trials and tribulation as He works to bring about changed character and hope (5:3-4).

God's love is poured out on us when we lose a loved one and as we walk through grief. He uses every second of our grief to develop perseverance. I found many things very difficult to accomplish after I lost a loved one. Sometimes, it was just getting the day started. Often, it was going somewhere by myself. I had always gone with that loved one to certain places, and now I was faced with doing it on my own. Other times, it was just being by myself with no one near. For instance, the first time I cut myself badly, I nearly panicked. How do I get the bleeding stopped? What if I can't? How do I bandage it without help? Minor things as I look back, but at the time, I felt overwhelmed. I pushed through all those new experiences with the Lord's help, and the result was perseverance.

Perseverance brings about proven character as we walk through grief and as we continue to persevere. Proven character is tested character; it is maturity. It is the result of experiencing a variety of events, responding in a positive way, until it becomes second nature. After I started my day off, many, many times, it was easier to get started. When I had done things by myself many times, it was easier to do them by myself. For example, I drove by myself from Ohio to California to see my brother. I had never gone that far by myself, but God was with me, and I made it. I did it two more times since then and am planning on another trip. When I solved problems by myself frequently enough, I knew I could do it again with the Lord's help. I am not mechanically inclined, another challenge, but I was able to figure some things out on my own. I wasn't sure I could do these things on my own, but after trying new things, trying to fix things, making large purchases, etc., I gained confidence that I could do things with the Lord's help. My character was developing, changing, and proven.

Proven character brings hope. This is not wishful hope, "I hope things will turn out; I hope I will make it." This is hope that is a sure thing: that God is with me and for me, that God is working in my life, that He has a future for me, that my hope is in heaven and eternal life.

In the midst of grief and tribulation, remember that God is working. He is pouring out His love for you and is working in you and through you to bring you through the grief to perseverance, to character, and to hope. Put your faith and hope in Him because He has great plans for you, though it may not seem like it at the time.

Celebrate the hope He brings in tribulation!

Lord, thank You that You are with me now. Though I see trials, show me hope. Show me You are with me and in me. Help me to trust You more, to be confident that I can face today and tomorrow because You promise to bring me through tribulation to hope. In the name of the One who is my only hope, Jesus, amen.

_____

_____

_____

_____

_____

_____

29

He Carries You

"I've carried you since your birth. I've taken care of you from the time you were born. Even when you're old, I'll take care of you. Even when your hair turns gray, I'll support you".

(Isaiah 46:3b-4a, GW)

I don't have many memories from childhood. I don't know why; maybe it's a long-term memory issue. However, there are a few precious memories I do have. I remember sitting on my mother's lap with my sister as she held us and read to us. I remember the comfort and joy of being held by her, completely safe and enjoying her presence, hearing her voice as she read stories from a book. I didn't know how precious that book was at the time. She was reading from a set of Childcraft books, orange in color, leather-bound. Recently, I found the payment coupon book showing that my parents had invested their money, a few dollars a month, to get those books. My mother ordered the books less than three months after I was born, and they paid $5.15 a month until they were paid for. Money was tight, but they knew the value of time and money spent on books that could be read to us and give lasting memories. I still have the whole set of books, plus the payment booklet, proof of sacrifice made.

I also remember the time my mother sent me to the local grocery store on my bike to get a couple of things she needed.

She didn't drive, and they didn't have an extra car anyway, so I went on my bicycle. On the way, I skidded through some gravel, my bike and I tumbled, and I scraped knees and elbow. I didn't know it, though, because I was on a mission that must be completed. I got up, continued to the store, and came home with the items. When I arrived, my mother was horrified by what she saw: scraped and bloody knees and elbow. She examined me and questioned me to be sure I was alright, cleaned me up, and cared for me. She didn't even check to see if the groceries were okay; she was interested in my well-being.

A more recent memory is of my graduation from a university with a doctoral degree. My mother was instrumental in that achievement. When I graduated with a master's degree, she asked me if I thought I might get my doctorate as well. I said, "No." At the time, I didn't see the need. Nevertheless, she planted the thought in my mind, and ten years later, there I was, graduating again. I remember the pride and love both parents exhibited at such an accomplishment. The wonder of this achievement is that neither my mom nor dad completed high school! They grew up during the depression when times were hard, and there was hardly enough money to put food on the table, let alone get a college degree. To be able to go so far under the loving influence of a mother (and father) is indescribable.

I share all of these memories to give a glimpse of how much Jesus cares for us. He cares for me, and He cares for you in such a special way because we are valuable to Him and loved so greatly by Him. He loves us like a mother holding her child on her lap, close to her breast, safe and secure, giving her child full attention. In fact, Jesus longs to gather us in His arms, "…the way a hen gathers her chicks under her wings…" (Matthew 23:37,

NASB). He cares for us like a mother who takes her daughter in her arms, cleans her wounds, examines her to make sure all is well. He looks at us with a heart full of love when He sees how we have matured and developed under His guidance, listened to Him speak, and followed His voice.

God loves us even more than a parent! Since the day we were born (and even before we were born), He has taken care of us; He has carried us. He promises to carry us and care for us throughout life until we are old and gray. He cares for us in good times and bad and carries us when we can't make it on our own strength. I love the "Footprints" poem. It illustrates God's care for us. It describes a dream in which the speaker in the poem sees two pairs of footprints in the sand as he walks through life. One pair belongs to God. At the point where life was at its worst, there is only one pair of footprints. God explains He didn't leave the person alone: that's when He carried him. That's what God does for us: He walks beside us through life, carrying us when we need to be carried.

God is there for you. He is beside you every moment of every day, comforting, caring, and encouraging. No matter what you are going through, He hasn't left you alone. He never will. He will be with you throughout this life, and eventually, He will carry you right into heaven, into His loving arms.

Trust Him. He carries you!

Jesus, thank You for Your love for me. Thank You that You care for me like a mother who holds her child in her arms, safe and secure, like one who consoles me when I'm hurt, like one who looks at me with love for me as I grow and mature. Thank You that You will never let me go. In the name of the One who loves me with an everlasting love, Jesus, amen.

30

Now What?

"I shall remember the deeds of the Lᴏʀᴅ; I will certainly remember Your wonders of old".

(Psalm 77:11, NASB)

You've been grieving for a couple weeks, or maybe a few months, or perhaps for several years. You ask yourself, *Where is God in all this?* The answer is He is still here; He is still with you. God is still God, He is still on the throne, He is still in control, and He still loves you. He doesn't change; He is the same yesterday, today, and forever. Think about His role in your life in the past, the present, and the future, forever.

Psalm 77:11 tells us to remember the deeds of the Lord, His wonders of old. That involves two spheres: what He has done throughout history and what He has done for you personally. I get great encouragement from all the accounts of what God has done from creation: His provision, such as the Israelite in the wilderness; His rescues, such as Noah's family in the ark; His deliverances, such as the Jews in the time of Esther; His comfort, such as the promises of a coming Messiah; and His miracles, such as Jesus healing the sick and raising the dead. I am also greatly encouraged in my present circumstances (including those associated with grief) by all that He has does for me: His provision, such as daily needs and strength; His rescues, such as lifting me up out of the quicksands of despair; His deliverances, such as my salvation in Jesus Christ; His comfort, such as holding me in His hands as I walk through grief; and His miracles, such as the way He saved me from death and disaster several times.

All the things the Lord has done for me in the past give me great confidence in His role for me in the present. He is still my provider, rescuer, deliverer, comforter, and miracle worker. When I awake in the morning with no energy or initiative, I know I can ask Him to provide those today. He gets me up, renews my strength, and at the end of the day, I have had His energy and strength to carry me through. When I discover I have forgotten to pay a bill, He is there to rescue me and make it right. When I make a wrong decision, He is there to deliver me from the consequences and help me find the way to fix it. When my grief is overwhelming, He is there to comfort me. And when I start to fret, He is there to give me the miracle of a peace that surpasses all understanding. God is the same today as He was yesterday. He is still here and still in control! He is ready to be all that you need Him to be.

He will be the same for you tomorrow and forever. He will be your provider: He will supply all your needs, physical, emotional, and spiritual. He will be your rescuer: when you can't even think straight, He will rescue and help you remember all the things you need to do. He will be your deliverer: He will keep the enemy away from you, even those who try to take advantage of your circumstances. He will be your comforter: He will continue to hold your hand and even carry you through your grief. He will be your miracle worker, giving you peace that is beyond anything you can imagine. He will continue to be what He has always been.

When you come to your last days on earth, He will continue, as He always has, to be your provider, giving you strength for your final days; your rescuer, saving you from fear and pain; your deliverer, freeing you from your earthly body; your comforter as you face your final days on earth; and your miracle-worker, transporting you to your eternal home in heaven. What a wondrous thought: He, who has been with you in the past and is with you now, will continue to be there in the future and through all eternity. He will not abandon you.

Now what? Keep trusting Him; He has proven Himself faithful, and He will remain faithful.

Lord, thank You that You never change. You have always been with me, You are with me now, and You will be with me throughout my life. I look forward to spending eternity with You. In the name of the Alpha and Omega, the first and the last, the beginning and the end, He who is, and who was, and who is to come, the Almighty, Jesus, our Lord, amen.

_____

_____

_____

_____

_____

_____

_____

Appendix A

Confidence in God/Peace of God

"Peace I leave with you, My peace I give to you; not as the world gives do I give to you. Let not your heart be troubled, neither let it be afraid". (John 14:27, NKJV).

"These things I have spoken to you, that in Me you may have peace. In the world you will have tribulation, but be of good cheer, I have overcome the world" (John 16:33, NKJV).

"Now may the God of hope fill you with all joy and peace in believing" (Romans 15:13, NKJV).

"God is not the author of confusion, but of peace" (1 Corinthians 14:33, NKJV).

"Be anxious for nothing, but in everything by prayer and supplication with thanksgiving, let your requests be made known to God; and the peace of God which surpasses all understanding, will guard your hearts and minds through Christ Jesus" (Philippians 4:6-7, NKJV).

"…let the peace of God rule in your hearts…and be thankful" (Colossians 3:15, NKJV).

"For God has not given us a spirit of fear, but of power and love and of a sound mind" (2 Timothy 1:7, NKJV).

"Now may the Lord of peace Himself give you peace always in every way" (2 Thessalonians 3:16, NKJV).

"Do not be afraid as you go out to fight your enemies today! Do not lose heart or panic or tremble before them. For the LORD your God is going with you! He will fight for you against your enemies, and He will give you victory" (Deuteronomy 20:3b-4, NLT).

"It is the LORD who goes before you. He will be with you; He will not leave you or forsake you. Do not fear or be dismayed" (Deuteronomy 31:8, ESV).

"Have I not commanded you? Be strong and courageous! Do not be terrified nor dismayed, for the LORD your God is with you wherever you go" (Joshua 1:9, NASB).

"Many are saying of me, 'God will not deliver him.' But you, LORD, are a shield around me, my glory, the One who lifts my head high" (Psalm 3:2-3, NIV).

"In peace I will lie down and sleep, for you alone, O LORD, will keep me safe" (Psalm 4:8, NLT).

"The LORD gives His people strength. The LORD blesses them with peace" (Psalm 29:11, NLT).

"Why, my soul, are you downcast? Why so disturbed within me? Put your hope in God, for I will yet praise Him, my Savior and my God" (Psalm 43:5, NIV).

"My health may fail, and my spirit grow weak, but God remains the strength of my heart; He is mine forever" (Psalm 73:26, NLT).

"I will hear what God the LORD will speak, For He will speak peace to His people and to His saints; But let them not turn back to folly" (Psalm 85:8, NKJV).

"I said to myself, 'Relax, because the LORD takes care of you'" (Psalm 116:7, NCV).

"As pressure and stress bear down on me, I find joy in your commands" (Psalm 119:143, NLT).

"Great peace have those who love Your law, and nothing causes them to stumble" (Psalm 119:165, NIV).

"My son, do not forget my teaching, but let you heart keep my commandments, for length of days and years of life and peace they will add to you" (Proverbs 3:1-2, ESV).

"Behold, God is my salvation, I will trust and not be afraid; For the LORD God is my strength and song, and He has become my salvation" (Isaiah 12:2, NASB).

"You will keep him in perfect peace, Whose mind is stayed on You, Because he trusts in You" (Isaiah 26:3, NKJV).

> Have you not known? Have you not heard? The everlasting God, the LORD, The Creator of the ends of the earth, neither faints nor is weary. His understanding is unsearchable. He gives power to the weak, and to those who have no might He increases strength. Even the youths shall faint and be weary, and the young men shall utterly fall, But those who wait on the LORD shall renew their strength; They shall mount up with wings like eagles, They shall run and not be weary, They shall walk and not faint.
>
> Isaiah 40:28-31 (NKJV)

"So do not fear, for I am with you; do not be dismayed for I am your God. I will strengthen you and help you; I will uphold you with My righteous right hand" (Isaiah 41:10, NIV).

"I am the LORD your God who takes hold of your right hand and says to you, Do not fear; I will help you" (Isaiah 41:13, NIV).

"When you pass through the waters, I will be with you; and through the rivers, they will not overflow you. When you walk through the fire, you will not be scorched, nor will the flame burn you. For I am the LORD you God, The Holy One of Israel, your Savior" (Isaiah 43:2-3a, NASB).

"Oh that you had heeded My commandments! Then your peace would have been like a river, And your righteousness, like the waves of the sea" (Isaiah 48:18, NKJV).

"For you shall go out in joy and be led forth in peace" (Isaiah 55:12a, ESV).

"This I recall to mind, Therefore I have hope. Through the LORD's mercies we are not consumed, because His compassions fail not. They are new every morning; great is Your faithfulness. 'The LORD is my portion,' says my soul, 'Therefore I hope in Him!'" (Lamentations 3:21-24, NKJV)

"The LORD your God in your midst, the Mighty One, will save; He will rejoice over you with gladness, He will quiet you with His love, He will rejoice over you with singing" (Zephaniah 3:17, NKJV).

About the Author

Linda was saved through the witness of a very dear friend during her senior year of college. She finished her degree in education and was immediately called to Christian ministry. She ministered for over three decades at a Christian school, where she served at various times as classroom teacher, special education teacher, assistant director of special education, principal, and director of curriculum and instruction. During that time, she completed her master's and doctorate degrees. She also ministered for five years as associate professor at Mount Vernon Nazarene University. In addition, she was actively involved with the Association of Christian Schools International, leading many workshops, assisting in the writing of their spelling book, and helping other Christian schools with the accreditation process. She served in the local church in various capacities, including Sunday school teacher, Awana leader, and Bible study leader. She is single and lives in Ohio with her dog, Annie.

CPSIA information can be obtained
at www.ICGtesting.com
Printed in the USA
BVHW070451301121
622779BV00008B/479